With Walker in Nicaragua

ERNESTO CARDENAL

With Walker in Nicaragua

AND OTHER EARLY POEMS, 1949–1954

**Selected and Translated by
JONATHAN COHEN**

WESLEYAN UNIVERSITY PRESS
Middletown, Connecticut

The translator is grateful to:

El Cid Editor for permission to use the Spanish original of "John Roach, marinero." Copyright © 1979 by EL CID EDITOR.

Cuadernos Latinoamericanos, Ediciones Carlos Lohlé, for permission to use the Spanish originals of "Raleigh," "Las mujeres nos quedaban mirando," "Viajero del Siglo XIX en el Río San Juan" (originally titled "El bongo mudo bogaba por el río"), "Los filibusteros," "Greytown," "Squier en Nicaragua," "Acuarela" and "León." Copyright © 1971 Carlos Lohlé, soc. anón. ind. y com.

Editorial Universitaria Centroamericana (EDUCA) for permission to use the Spanish originals of "Con Walker en Nicaragua," "Estrella encontrada muerta en Park Avenue," "José Dolores Estrada," "Joaquín Artola," and "Omagua." Copyright © 1972 Editorial Universitaria Centroamericana (EDUCA), Organización de las Universidades Nacionales Autónomas de Costa Rica, Guatemala, El Salvador, Honduras y Nicaragua.

The editors of the following journals, who published some of these translations: *The American Poetry Review* ("The Filibusters," "Greytown," "John Roach, Mariner"), *The Denver Quarterly* ("Squier in Nicaragua"), *Ironwood* ("With Walker in Nicaragua"), *The Nation* ("León"), *New Directions in Prose and Poetry* ("Raleigh," "Star Found Dead on Park Avenue"), and *Street Magazine* ("José Dolores Estrada").

All inquiries and permissions requests should be addressed to the Publisher, Wesleyan University Press, 110 Mt. Vernon Street, Middletown, Connecticut 06457.

Distributed by Harper & Row Publishers, Keystone Industrial Park, Scranton, Pennsylvania 18512.

LIBRARY OF CONGRESS CATALOGING IN PUBLICATION DATA

Cardenal, Ernesto.
    With Walker in Nicaragua and other early poems (1949-1954)

Wesleyan Poetry in Translation
    1. Cardenal, Ernesto—Translations, English.
I. Cohen, Jonathan. II. Title.
PQ7519.C34A23 1985   861   84-7480
ISBN 0-8195-5123-6 (alk. paper)
ISBN 0-8195-6118-5 (pbk. : alk. paper)

Manufactured in the United States of America

WESLEYAN PAPERBACK, FIRST PRINTING, 1984
SECOND PRINTING, 1985

Contents

Acknowledgments

I would like to thank the National Endowment for the Arts, which awarded me a grant to translate these poems, and the National Endowment for the Humanities, which awarded me a grant to do the research for the introductory essay. I would also like to thank M. L. Rosenthal, Conrad Kent, Hugh Harter, David Unger, and Hardie St. Martin for their generous criticism of translations in manuscript. In addition, grateful acknowledgment is made to Robert Bly for his translation of the opening lines of Rubén Darío's "To Roosevelt."

JONATHAN COHEN

With Walker in Nicaragua

Introduction

FROM NICARAGUA WITH LOVE

*Hunter, the only way to approach you
is with a voice like that of the Bible, or poems
like those of Walt Whitman.*

—Darío in "To Roosevelt"

Ernesto Cardenal is not only the best-known living writer of Nicaragua, but also probably the most widely read poet writing in Spanish today. He has produced a body of verse that spans from the nineteen-forties to the present. His mature work marks the emergence of a realist, or concrete, poetry (as opposed to the surrealist or abstract) in Latin America, representing a reaction against an excessively subjective literary tradition. It is, moreover, the work of a poet committed to social justice and human dignity. Viewed chronologically, together with his earliest poems, it reveals his development as a poet motivated by an ever-widening notion of love: at first of women; then of the tropics, the lakes, everything that is Nicaragua; and finally of God. Indeed, Cardenal's quest for love—for communion—has played a key role in shaping both his life and his poetry.

Cardenal was born in 1925 in Granada, on the northern shore of Lake Nicaragua. In 1930 his family moved to León, the city where Rubén Darío, the founder of modern Spanish American poetry, had lived. Cardenal recalls: "Rubén... was a very devout boy who went to confession every Saturday at the Church of St. Francis. Likewise, I went to confession every Saturday at the same church."

I used to live in a big house by the Church of St. Francis
which had an inscription in the entrance hall saying
AVE MARIA
and red corridors of brick,

an old red-tiled roof,
                    and windows with rusty iron grilles,
and a large courtyard just unbearable on stuffy afternoons
with a sad clock bird singing out the hours,
and someone's pale aunt in the courtyard reciting the rosary.

In León he read Darío's poetry at the age of eleven, and the first poem he remembers writing, at age seven, was an homage to Darío.

The first significant phase of Cardenal's poetic development dates from roughly 1940 to 1946. The poems he composed during these years echo the major Latin American poets of the time, and he has said: "When I was eighteen, Neruda exerted the greatest influence on the poetry I was writing.... But the influence of Vallejo was more profound, not so much on my literary style, but on my soul." Cardenal's earliest efforts were in traditional verse forms, but by the mid-forties he was writing in free verse with a great degree of lyricism and subjectivity. For the most part he explored themes of romantic love, often attempting to gain emotional intensity through an excessive use of descriptive language. His first collection, "Carmen y otros poemas" ("Carmen and Other Poems"), was written from 1943 to 1945, and never published. It includes poems expressing his search for identity, as well as for a "heaven on earth" found through love. Three poems that reveal the style and temperament of the "Carmen" work appeared in 1946 in a popular Mexican journal: "Amor irremediable" ("Incurable Love"), "Amor que pasa y no vuelve" ("Love That Goes By and Doesn't Come Back") and "Egloga inconsolable" ("Downhearted Eclogue"). Though today he considers this adolescent writing highly derivative and not worthy of publication, it demonstrates a movement toward two distinctive features of his mature work: concreteness of imagery, especially visual imagery, and rhythms based on the qualitative nature of the subject matter.

One of the strongest efforts from the initial phase of Cardenal's development is the long poem entitled "La ciudad deshabitada" ("The Deserted City"), which was written in 1946 in the aftermath of a broken love affair. It opens this way:

Besieged by the deaths of all its afternoons forever,
on that land white as the salt on which it was founded,
white as thirst, in the desolation of the sun,
and the death rattle of a lake that by noon feels like ash,
motionless, motionless, all the way out to its horizon,
like a slab of stone fit perfectly to the infinite,
and those waves going through an unceasing graveyard,
often by myself I remember all the streets,
often in sleep my body has gone through them once more,
and so at night it emerges, entirely white,
in the midst of the land on which its ruin has been built.
Besieged by dust, by time slowly invading the stone,
a defeated city that we have to flee,
because here a final ash has joined the assault,
because here nothing remains and we have to leave,
we have to leave. But something comes back,
at certain unexplainable times just after it rains,
or when we sleep beneath long-absent skies,
or we resume a conversation left hanging years ago,
something comes back, something can't leave for good,
and so we call excitedly to some precious door
that opened in the evening to a hundred dreams of love.

The other transitional poem that should be noted here is "Proclama del conquistador" ("The Conquistador's Proclamation"), which was written the following year, and which achieves apparent objectivity through the use of third-person narrative. Moreover, the "Proclamation" reveals Cardenal's shift from personal to historical themes, and previews the hallmark of his writing ever since, namely, verse based on history.

The turning point in Cardenal's poetic development took place in New York, when he was attending Columbia University from late 1947 to late 1949. At Columbia he immersed himself in the poetry of North Americans, including Williams,

Fearing, Frost, Sandburg, and, above all, Pound, whom he has called his "main teacher." He began to adapt certain technical devices of these poets as he developed his own poetic style, for which he later coined the name *exteriorismo* to describe "poetry created with images from the world around us [*el mundo exterior*] ...an objective poetry: narrative and anecdotal, made with elements from real life, with concrete things, proper names and precise details, exact dates and figures and facts and statements." It was during the formative years in New York, in the spring of 1949, that Cardenal wrote "Raleigh," his first *exteriorista* poem and, in his opinion, the earliest poem that represents his mature voice—precisely the kind of voice Pound had expected: poetry not trying "to seem forcible by rhetorical din, and luxurious riot...[with] fewer painted adjectives impeding the shock and stroke of it...austere, direct, free of emotional slither."

In New York Cardenal first lived on the top floor of a twelve-story apartment house near Columbia. He had a small place in which he was surrounded by books and magazines, Mexican images painted on tin and carved gourds from Nicaragua on the walls, with his typewriter and a little radio. Later, he took a small room at International House, a residence for foreign and American graduate students on the Upper West Side. He had an active social life within and outside Columbia's world. He had girl friends—girls were always a big part of his youth, part of what has been called his "love affair with love." He explored the whole city, and in his long poem "Trip to New York," written after a visit twenty-three years later, the memories come back:

Central Park (uptown): And I tell myself: that's where the swans are.
I remember my Liana, and the swans.
She got married. The swans must still be there.
Once, one hungry day, Louis trying to catch a swan.

Once again I saw people talking to themselves in the streets
            "The Lonely Crowd."

At Columbia he studied British and American literature; among his professors were Lionel Trilling, Carl Van Doren, and Babette Deutsch. But, most important, in New York Cardenal began to identify himself as a poet.

Although he wrote only three poems in New York—"Raleigh," "The Women Kept Looking at Us" and "Omagua"—he initiated his rediscovery of the New World.* The poems that followed in the next few years would have, as the Nicaraguan poet Pablo Antonio Cuadra says, "a common denominator: the vision of America from a foreign eye." Cardenal has used the eye of explorers, travelers, journalists and adventurers for recovering the wonderment and otherness of his world. And, like Pound, he has used documentary sources, crosscutting from source to source, and making a kind of verse montage that attains a lyric or epic movement of energy and whose grace lies in the cuts and seams of the poems.

In the fall of 1949, Cardenal left New York for several months of study in Europe. He went to Paris and Madrid, making friends with other poets and writers. He toured Italy and Switzerland, too. Recording his observations of the Old World in a journal, he would later draw on them to compose a sequence of short imagistic poems entitled "Postales europeas" ("European Postcards"):

Behind the flowered-iron balconies,
                    the rosy sea.
Striped awnings and colorful umbrellas,

---

*Cardenal wrote the first version of "Star Found Dead on Park Avenue" in New York in 1949. Some twenty years later he produced the final, more amplified, version, which appears in this collection. It is the only poem written in New York based on his personal experience there.

and voices of girls on a tennis court
                    under laurel trees.

And then in July 1950, after three fertile years abroad, at the age of twenty-five, he finally went home.

Back in Nicaragua, Cardenal settled in Managua, the capital city. He wrote "With Walker in Nicaragua" just after his return. Having used colonial history in previous efforts, he now turned to more recent history, specifically, the Filibuster War of 1855–57 and its central figure, William Walker of Tennessee. Though lost in American history today, Walker's exploits in Nicaragua were big news in the mid-nineteenth century; in fact, according to the historian Frederic Rosengarten, Jr., "he was the hottest news personality between the discovery of gold in California and the Civil War." For a time the most talked about man in the United States, Walker was called the "Grey-Eyed Man of Destiny," and was also known as the "king of the fili-busters," the Yankee mercenaries or freebooters with whom he had invaded Nicaragua. Starting with fifty-seven men (later called the "Immortals"), Walker soon had an army of thousands and made himself President of Nicaragua—men flocked to the filibuster army from all over America. He was at first helped by Cornelius Vanderbilt, who ran a prosperous shipping line to California via Nicaragua. Walker hoped to make Nicaragua a powerful slave state, and to build an empire. His grand design was to attach Central America and Cuba to the Slave States. As President of Nicaragua, he legalized slavery, issued bonds, made English the official language, and finally alienated Vanderbilt (Walker had revoked his transit company concession). The com-bined forces of the five Central American republics, supported by Great Britain and Vanderbilt, succeeded in driving him out. He made three attempts to return, but was finally captured and executed in Honduras.

Not surprisingly, Walker is still remembered well in Central

America, where schoolchildren read about his quest for power. "With Walker in Nicaragua" tells the story of Walker's rise and fall from the point of view of a sympathetic old man, a filibuster in his youth, whom Cardenal has created out of several different sources:

In a lonely cabin on the frontier,
I, Clinton Rollins, attempting no literary style,
pass the time by penning my memories.
And as an old man my thoughts wander back:

The things that happened fifty years ago...

Spanish Americans I have known
        —whom I have grown to like...
And that warm, sweet, green odor of Central America.
The white houses with red-tiled roofs and with wide sunny eaves,
and a tropical courtyard with a fountain and a woman by the fountain.
And the heat making our beards grow longer.
What scenes return to my memory now!
A grey wave that comes blotting out the hills
and a muffled sound of flood waters rushing through the jungle
and the howls of monkeys on the opposite bank
and then the heavy, metallic beating of raindrops on the tin roofs
and the people running to take in the clothes from the ranch porches
and later the grey wave and the muffled sound moving off
and once again the silence...
And how it smelled of underbrush and the river turned leaf-green,
how the little steamboat looked there, calm as could be,
anchored to the shade of the jungle.
And the sudden flop of an iguana into the water,
the rumble of falling timber,
the distant shot of a rifle,
a Spanish word shouted from afar,
the laughter of the black women washing clothes
and a Caribbean song.

In later poems he makes allusions to Walker, who personifies this chapter in the mutual history of the United States and Nicaragua, as in the revolutionary classic "Hora O" ("Zero Hour"). When recounting the dictator's murder of Augusto César Sandino, the guerrilla leader who fought against the intervention of the U.S. Marines in the late twenties and early thirties, Cardenal says:

And meanwhile in the drawing rooms of the Presidential Palace
and in the prison yards and in the barracks
and the American Embassy and the Police Station
those who stood guard that night saw one another in the ghostly dawn
with hands and faces as though stained with blood.

"*I did it,*" Somoza said later.
"*I did it, for the good of Nicaragua.*"

And William Walker said when they were about to kill him:
"The President of Nicaragua is a Nicaraguan."

"With Walker in Nicaragua" shows Cardenal's notion of love broadening. He had come to embrace his homeland, its people, culture and landscape. As an expression of this love, soon after his return to Nicaragua, he began to take part in the political struggle against the dynastic tyranny of Anastasio Somoza. He joined an illegal group of young revolutionaries called the UNAP (Unión Nacional de Acción Popular, or National Union of Popular Action), and over the next few years frequently wrote articles against the government for the country's major newspaper, *La Prensa,* whose publisher, it should be noted, was one of the founders of the UNAP, as well as a member of Cardenal's family.

Despite his growing political activity, Cardenal was still very much engaged with poetry. Around 1951 he realized his dream of setting up a poetry press, with the help of the poet José Coronel Urtecho. The press was named El Hilo Azul (The Blue Thread). It was small but energetic, until it folded a couple years later, and, in view of the repressive political climate in Nicaragua at the time, it was a kind of revolutionary act in itself. Its first book was a translation of selected works by various American poets titled *Lincoln de los poetas* (Lincoln of the Poets). Cardenal had collaborated with Coronel on translating poems by Whitman, Masters, Bynner, Sandburg, Lindsay and others, which shared the theme of the memory of Lincoln, whom Cardenal considered the most poetic and heroic figure in U.S. history. But the majority of El Hilo Azul's publications, with forewords by Cardenal, were devoted to Nicaraguan poets. The office of the press became a meeting place for poets—and for UNAP members as well.

Cardenal's literary efforts grew along with his political engagement. He was busy preparing a manuscript of his poems for publication, to be his first book, but this collection never came out. Nonetheless, he was establishing himself as an important young poet; in 1952 "With Walker in Nicaragua" won the prize of the Managua Centenary. He continued to produce New World poems based on nineteenth-century history, such as "The Filibusters," "Joaquín Artola," "José Dolores Estrada" and "Greytown." Inspired by Pound's translations from the classics, he was also translating epigrams of Catullus and Martial, and writing his own epigrams, the earliest of which were stinging love poems. Then as he became more deeply involved with revolutionary politics, his epigrams became more political. For this reason they went underground, circulating in mimeographed form, anonymously. Beyond Nicaragua, they were read in Mexico, Guatemala, Cuba and Colombia, and Neruda published some in Chile, without knowing who had written them. About his epigrams Cardenal points out: "There is more to life than revolution. There is also love. My epigrams . . . are a poetry of love and hate, some of love and hate at the same time, because while they are political poems they are also love poems." Here is one of them:

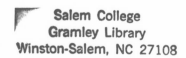

They told me you were in love with another man
and then I went off to my room
and I wrote that article against the Government
that landed me in this jail.

The epigrams demonstrate Cardenal's increasing ability to con-
dense complex relationships into a single, hard and clear image
—again, precisely what his "main teacher," Pound, had expect-
ed: "dichten = condensare." They also demonstrate Cardenal's
mastery of understatement, as well as a sense of humor which
often saves his poetry from falling into rhetorical bombast.
According to him, the epigrams reflect his two main passions in
the early fifties, namely, "girls and revolutionary politics." Both
passions are subtly expressed in "Squier in Nicaragua." Finished
in 1954, the long poem portrays Nicaragua in the 1850s. It
likens Nicaragua to the Nicaraguan women exploited by the
gold-rushers passing through the country, heading for Califor-
nia. At the same time it celebrates Nicaragua in lyrical passages
that evoke the beauty of the country's lush jungles, lakes, towns
and women.

In 1954 Cardenal's political activities of the preceding four
years culminated in his participation in an attempted revolt,
later known as the "April Conspiracy." He had learned how to
handle a machine gun, and on the night of April 3, he joined an
assault on the Presidential Palace. Due to last-minute treachery
within the ranks of the conspirators, the revolt failed. Most of
the main leaders were captured, interrogated under torture and
killed; many other conspirators were imprisoned or forced into
exile or they simply "disappeared" in the custody of the National
Guard. Though Cardenal was lucky enough to avoid arrest, he
lived in fear of being caught:

Oh, to be able to sleep in your own bed tonight

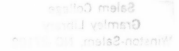

without the fear of being roused and taken out of your house,
the fear of knocks on the door or doorbells ringing in the night!

The violence he had experienced haunted him. Over the next
two years he suffered a growing feeling of emptiness. He wrote
more angry epigrams and the long "Zero Hour," a major section
of which recounts the events of the "April Conspiracy."

Cardenal came to feel that his love relationships with women
—Claudia, Myriam and Ileana—could not satisfy him. "In
reality," he says, "my obsession with love was a hunger for an
absolute, for an infinite love that human love cannot satisfy, but
I did not understand this." He adds:

Sometimes at night, in moments of solitude, especially after a party or
carousing with friends, I faced myself, and felt a hidden anguish. . . . It was
as though within me I were hearing the voice of a scornful love. I was
convinced God loved me, wanting me for Himself, with a jealous, tyranni-
cal love. But I pretended to be deaf. However, the voice persisted, over the
years. One day I couldn't stand it anymore. I felt harassed too much by that
Lover, whom I didn't love and who wanted me to love only Him, and I
made up my mind to give in, to see what would happen.

The result was a great religious awakening. Toward the end of
1956 he decided to meet this "Lover." He then wrote to Our
Lady of Gethsemani, the monastery in Kentucky that during
his New York days he had read about in the books of the Trappist
writer Thomas Merton. Cardenal was finding his way to love
humanity as a whole, and to serve God. It was, ironically, as
though he had finally found the way he longed for in one of his
earliest poems entitled "La casa de Cristo" ("The House of
Christ"), written when he was about fifteen:

Show me where you live and in which house,
or tell me at least on which street,
which way I must go to find you
and which house or park is by your house.

And so, in 1957, he entered the Trappist monastery at Gethsemani, where he became a disciple of Merton. Interestingly, to answer the question about his current profession when applying to the monastery, he wrote, "Poet."

For reasons of health Cardenal had to leave the monastery after two years. He continued his studies in Mexico and Colombia. In 1965 he returned to Nicaragua, at the urging of Merton, and was ordained a priest. In the same year he founded a small contemplative community which he named Nuestra Señora de Solentiname (Our Lady of Solentiname); Solentiname is an archipelago of thirty-eight islands located in the remote southern part of Lake Nicaragua, where about a thousand peasants live. Cardenal explains:

Contemplation means union with God. We soon realized that this union with God was leading us to union with the very poor, forgotten peasant farmers who lived along the banks of the archipelago. This same contemplation soon led us to political engagement. Contemplation led us to the revolution. And so it had to be; otherwise, it would have been false contemplation. My old novice master, Thomas Merton, had told me that in Latin America contemplation could not be divorced from the political struggle.

The community became internationally known for its efforts to practice the gospel, as well as for the school of "naïve" painting that developed there.

In the meantime, Cardenal's fame as a poet was spreading throughout Latin America and the rest of the world. He believed that his two vocations, poetry and priesthood, went hand in hand. For him, poetry came to mean "prophecy in the Biblical sense of guidance." He had published *Epigramas*, his first book, in 1961. *Salmos (Psalms)*, *Gethsemani, Ky.* and *Oración por Marilyn Monroe y otros poemas* (Prayer for Marilyn Monroe and Other Poems) appeared in the next few years. The books he published after founding Our Lady of Solentiname would continue to express his New World love and his commitment to the radical ideals of the "theology of liberation": *El estrecho dudoso* (The Dubious Strait), *Homenaje a los indios americanos* (*Homage to the American Indians*), *Canto nacional* (National Canto), *Oráculo sobre Managua* (Oracle over Managua), and several anthologies of his poetry.

Though he seldom left his retreat in Solentiname, he went to Cuba in 1970 to serve on the jury of a poetry contest. He spent three months there, during which time he found Cuba to be well on the way to realizing what he considered an ideal society —all that it essentially lacked in his view was a sound Christian basis. Much inspired by the socialist state, he felt that in Cuba "the Vallejo-era of America had begun (the new man, and man brother of man)," and his account of Cuba's virtues and defects is related in a prose work titled *En Cuba* (*In Cuba*).

In 1977, in response to the revolutionary activities of Cardenal and members of his community, Somoza destroyed Our Lady of Solentiname. Forced into exile in Costa Rica, Cardenal became a roving ambassador and later also a field chaplain for the FSLN (Frente Sandinista de Liberación Nacional, or Sandinist National Liberation Front), the revolutionary group that finally overthrew Somoza in 1979:

And now at last the beach at Poneloya, and the plane
                             coming in to land,
the string of foam along the coast gleaming in the moonlight.
       The plane coming down. A smell of insecticide.
And Sergio tells me: "The smell of Nicaragua!"
It's the most dangerous moment, enemy aircraft
            may be waiting for us over the airport.
And the airport lights at last.
We've landed. From out of the dark come our fatigue-clad comrades
to greet us with hugs.
We feel their warm bodies, that also come from the sun,
that also are light.
       This revolution is fighting the darkness.

It was daybreak on July 18th. And the beginning
of all that was about to come.

In that year Cardenal was named Minister of Culture of the new
government. He has continued to hold this position for the past
five years. He explains:

My job is to promote everything cultural in Nicaragua. I have a ministry of
poetry, music, painting, crafts, theater, folklore and tradition, and schol-
arly research, which includes libraries, magazines, films and recreation. I
think of my ministry this way: just as Christ put his apostles in charge of
distributing the loaves and fishes, he has put me in charge of spreading
culture. The people do not consume culture, they create it. This is what I
did in Solentiname, only now I do it country-wide.

He regards as one of his most successful projects the poetry
workshops in which writers from all walks of life make use of
rules on poetic technique he gleaned from Pound's *Guide to
Kulchur* and *ABC of Reading.* But despite the many new forms
of progress in Nicaragua, the Sandinist victory did not end
political strife within the country—*La Prensa* remains an op-
position newspaper, subject to censorship—and Cardenal's role
in the controversial government, now criticized throughout the
world, awaits the final judgment of history.

Today, Cardenal is considered the most outstanding socially
committed poet to appear in Latin America since Neruda. His
books have been translated into all the major modern languages.
In 1980 he was awarded the prestigious Peace Prize of the
German Publishers Association for a canon revealing "love as
an essential element of social change"; the first Latin American
to receive the prize, he accepted it not for himself, but for the
great and courageous people of Nicaragua. Commenting on *ex-
teriorismo,* the esthetic that has guided him ever since he com-
posed "Raleigh," Cardenal maintains that it is "the only poetry

capable of expressing the Latin American reality... of being good for something: for building a nation, and creating a new man, changing society, making the future Nicaragua, as part of the great future homeland that is Latin America."

JONATHAN COHEN

A Note on Translation

I have tried to produce a faithful paraphrase of Cardenal's poetry. I have worked at bearing his utterance into my own, using language that I (as he) always could, in some circumstance, in the stress of some emotion, actually say. Moreover, approaching translation as an act of sympathy, I have done my best to convey the poetic quality of his work through living poems in English.

Most of the poems in this collection are based on documentary sources, including old chronicles, magazine articles and personal narratives, often originally written in English. Whenever possible, I have used them to shed light on Cardenal's poetry, and to suppply certain language for my translation. "Squier in Nicaragua" offers a good example of how Cardenal has used a documentary source, and how I, in turn, have used the same source in the critical/creative process of translation. The poem is based on Ephraim George Squier's treatise titled *Nicaragua; Its People, Scenery, Monuments, and the Proposed Interoceanic Canal*, published in 1852; Squier, an American journalist, archaeologist and diplomat, had traveled throughout Nicaragua, recording his observations and experiences, which are presented in his book about the country.

The poem opens with a panoramic sequence of images portraying Nicaragua's tropical landscape with its "green afternoons in the jungle; sad / afternoons." The opening sequence culminates with an image for which Cardenal draws on Squier's description of "a very pretty yellow girl, swinging to and fro in a hammock, with one naked leg hanging indolently over the side." Squier adds that as he glanced into her hut, "she threw aside her long black curls, but, without changing her position, exclaimed, 'Adios, California!' " Cardenal, then, adapts Squier in the following verse:

Una muchacha meciéndose en una hamaca,
con su largo pelo negro, y una pierna desnuda
colgando de la hamaca,
nos saluda:
      "Adiós, California!"

And my translation reads:

A girl swinging to and fro in a hammock,
with long black hair, and a bare leg
hanging out of the hammock,
greets us:
      "Adios, California!"

I have not followed Squier slavishly in translating Cardenal. Doing so would be a mistake because the purpose of the verse adaptation is far from that of the prose. But like Cardenal, I have drawn freely on what Squier says. In addition, when appropriate I have used *how* Squier says what he does; for instance, his using the Spanish "Adios, California!" My translation thus attempts to express a fidelity not just to Cardenal's words but to his method of composition as well.

Before bowing out to let the translations speak for themselves, I wish to acknowledge my personal indebtedness to Cardenal. He has generously taken part in the process of translation, reviewing my drafts with great care, and clarifying for me the sense of certain words and phrases, in particular the Nicaraguanisms. Furthermore, he has helped me to do this translation with special confidence because he himself feels that I achieve my principal goal: to translate his poems as though he were originally writing them in English.

JONATHAN COHEN

Finding the Voice

Raleigh

Al este del Perú, hacia el mar, en la línea del Equinoccio
sobre un lago blanco, salado, de doscientas leguas de largo
está Manoa,
Manoa, mansión del sol, espejo de la luna,
Manoa que Juan Martín había visto un día
cuando le quitaron ante ella la venda al mediodía
y anduvo todo ese día hasta la noche por en medio de la ciudad.
Y yo sabía de ella desde hacía tiempo por relatos
cómo riela de noche en el lago como luna
y el resplandor del oro al mediodía.
Todo el servicio de su casa, mesa y cocina era de oro
dice Gomara
y hallaron cincuenta y dos mil marcos de buena plata
y un millón y trescientos y veinte y seis mil y quinientos
pesos de oro,
dice del tesoro de Atahualpa en el Cuzco,
que hallaron cincuenta y dos mil marcos de buena plata
y un millón y trescientos y veinte y seis mil y quinientos pesos de oro.
¡Porque dijeron que las piedras que trajimos no eran oro!
Y yo conversaba con los caciques en sus casas
y daba vino en Trinidad a los españoles para que hablaran.
Y yo supe todos los ríos y los reinos;
desde la frontera del Perú hasta el Mar del Este,
desde el Orinoco hacia el sur hasta el Amazonas
y la región de María Tamball,
todos los reinos.
Y la vida que en ellos se hace, y sus costumbres.
Orenqueponi, Taparimaca, Winicapora.
Era como si los estuviera viendo.

Raleigh

Due east from Peru, towards the sea, by the Equinoctial Line,
upon a white lake of salt water 200 leagues long
lies Manoa,
Manoa, mansion of the sun, mirror of the moon,
Manoa that Juan Martín had seen one day
when at noon as he entered it they removed his blindfold
and he traveled all that day till night through the city.
I knew about it for years from reports
how it glimmers at night on the moony lake
and the splendor of the gold at noon.
All the vessels of his house, table, and kitchen, were of gold
says Gomara
and they found 52,000 marks of good silver, and 1,326,500
pesos of gold,
he says about the treasure of Atahualpa in Cuzco,
that they found 52,000 marks of good silver
and 1,326,500 pesos of gold.
For they said that the stones we brought were not gold!
And I spoke with the caciques in their houses
and gave wine to the Spaniards in Trinidad to get them talking.
And I learned about all the rivers and kingdoms;
from the East Sea to the borders of Peru,
from the Orinoco southwards as far as the Amazon
and the region of María Tamball,
all the kingdoms.
And the way of life that's followed in them, and their customs.
Orenqueponi, Taparimaca, Winicapora.
It was as if I were seeing them.

(*Note:* This poem is based on Raleigh's account of his "discovery of the large, rich, and
beautiful empire of Guiana; with a relation of the great and golden city of Manoa,
which the Spaniards call El Dorado.")

Los indios de las costas, los de las islas, los Caníbales,
Caníbales de Guanipe,
los indios llamados Assawai, Coaca, Aiai,
los Tuitas sobre los árboles, los Sin Cabeza
y al norte del Orinoco los Wikiri
y al sur de la boca del Orinoco los Arwaca
y más allá los Caníbales
y al sur las Amazonas.
Y entramos en Abril
cuando las reinas del Amazonas se juntan en las márgenes
y danzan desnudas y untadas de bálsamo y oro
hasta el fin de esa luna—
Entramos en Abril
los barcos muy lejos de nosotros anclados en el mar,
a la ventura—
100 hombres con sus balsas y sus provisiones para un mes
durmiendo bajo la lluvia
y el mal tiempo y al aire libre y bajo el sol ardiente
y las plantas pegadas en la piel y las ropas mojadas
y el sudor de tantos hombres juntos y el calor del sol—
(y yo que me acordaba de la Corte)
y una tristeza que al atardecer iba subiendo y el zumbido de los pantanos
y oíamos llorar de miedo los monos en la noche,
el grito de un animal asustado por otro
y el rumor de unos remos,
el roce de unas hojas en el río,
el paso de pezuñas suaves sobre hojas.
Voces: la tristeza de esas voces...
No existe en Inglaterra prisión tan solitaria.

Y el pan ya muy poco. Y nada de agua.

Las noches en lechos colgantes bajo el cielo del Brasil—
esa clase de camas que ellos llaman "hamacas"—

The Indians along the shores, those on the islands, the Cannibals,
Cannibals of Guanipa,
the Indians called Assawai, Coaca, Aiai,
the Tuitas dwelling on trees, the Headless Ones
and the Wikiri north of the Orinoco
and the Arwaca south of the mouth of the Orinoco
and beyond them, the Cannibals
and south of them, the Amazons.
And so we set out in April
when queens of the Amazons gather at the borders
and dance naked, anointed with balsam and gold,
till the finish of that moon—
We set out in April
our ships quite a long way from us anchored at sea,
on the venture—
100 men with their bags and their supplies for a month
sleeping out in the rain
and bad weather and in the open air and in the burning sun
and plants getting stuck to their skin and the wet clothes
and the sweat of so many men together and the sun's heat—
(and I who remembered the Court)
and a sadness growing heavier by late afternoon and the buzzing from
    the swamps
and we'd hear monkeys at night crying filled with fear,
the scream of an animal frightened by another
and the noise of some oars,
the plash of some leaves in the river,
the step of gentle hooves upon leaves.
Voices: the sadness of those voices...
No prison so lonely exists in England.

And already very little bread. And not a drop of water.

Nights in cots hanging under the sky of Brazil—
that kind of bed they call "hamacas"—

oyendo la corriente roncando en la oscuridad
y el tambor de tribu a tribu sobre los montes
y el rumor del agua subiendo.

Sin pan. Sin agua.
Los oídos aturdidos de silencio.
Los árboles tan altos que no sentíamos aire.
Y el rumor del agua subiendo.

Sin pan. Sin agua.
Sino tan sólo el agua gruesa y turbada del río.
Y hay un río rojo y con flujo que cuando el sol se pone es venenoso
y se le oye quejarse mientras no hay sol, y está enfermo.
Y unas lagunas negras y espesas, como brea...
Y el calor al acercarnos a la Línea.
Y el olor a hoja mojada y el sabor del cansancio.
Y de raudal en raudal, de cascada en cascada,
la risa al anochecer de la virgen verde del río
y el choque del agua con el agua.

Y el aire desfallecido. Y la selva solitaria...

La compañía comenzando a desesperarse.
¡Y a un día de la tierra donde se obtiene todo lo que se quiere!
Y en las riberas, flores y frutas maduras y verdes.
Y unos pájaros verdes—
largo tiempo nos divertíamos viéndolos pasar—
Y frutas de pan y monos y el pájaro Campana
y un aroma dulce de bálsamo y cinamomo
y la cera que derramaba el árbol Karamana
y el sudor de las selvas de sándalo y alcanfor:
los árboles manaban leche y miel,
manaban ámbar y gomas aromáticas—
y una fruta que estallaba con estrépito—

hearing the current rushing in the darkness
and the drum from tribe to tribe up in the mountains
and the roar of water growing louder.

No bread. No water.
Except for the murky water of the river, that's all.
The trees so high we couldn't feel the air.
And the roar of water growing louder.

No bread. No water.
Except for the murky water of the river, that's all.
And there's a red river that turns poisonous when the sun sets
and while the sun is down one hears it groan, and get sick.
And some lagoons black and thick, like tar...
And the heat as we drew towards the Line.
And the smell of wet leaves and the taste of weariness.
And from rapids to rapids, from cascade to cascade,
the laughter at nightfall of the green virgin of the river
and the crashing of water into water.

And the air weakening. And the jungle lonely...

My company beginning to lose hope.
And a day short of the land where all one desires is found!
And on the banks, flowers and ripe green fruits.
And some green birds —
we amused ourselves a good while watching them pass —
And breadfruits and monkeys and the Campana bird
and the sweet fragrance of balsam and soapberry
and the wax that the Karamana tree secretes
and the moisture in those jungles of sandalwood and camphor:
the trees were abounding in milk and honey,
they were abounding in amber and fragrant gums —
and some fruit that would burst with a bang —

desde lejos la oíamos de noche reventando.
Y hojas del tamaño de canoas caían sobre el río.
Y vimos la Montaña de Cristal, la vimos lejos,
levantada sobre el horizonte como una iglesia de plata
y un río caía de su cima con el clamor de mil campanas.
Y las hijas del Orinoco riendo entre los árboles...
Y cascadas que de lejos brillaban como ciudades,
como el humo que se alzara de un gran pueblo
y el retumbo y los truenos y el rebotar de las aguas.
Y yo no vi nunca una tierra mejor:
los verdes valles vacíos,
los pájaros cantando contra la tarde en cada árbol,
los ciervos que venían mansos al agua como al silbo de un amo
y el aire fresco del este
y el brillo de las piedras de oro bajo el sol.

15 días después divisamos con gran júbilo Guayana
y una fuerta ráfaga de viento sopló del norte esa tarde
y llegamos de noche a un sitio en que el río se abre en tres brazos
y anclamos esa noche bajo las estrellas sintiendo el aroma de Guayana.
¡La cercanía de la tierra de Guayana!
Pero tuvimos que regresarnos hacia el este
porque empezaron las lluvias: aquellos grandes diluvios
y los ríos inundados, y pantanos sin fin—
dejando atrás Guayana con su espada de fuego,
dejando Guayana con el sol a quien adora.
Y entramos otra vez al mar, tristes...

from afar we'd hear it at night exploding.
And leaves big as canoes would fall upon the river.
And we saw the Crystal Mountain, we saw it afar off,
standing on the horizon like a silver church
and a river fell from its tip with a terrible noise like a thousand bells.
And the daughters of the Orinoco laughing amid the trees...
And cascades that shone from afar like cities,
like a smoke rising over some great town
and the rumble and thunder and rebounding of the waters.
I never saw a more beautiful country:
the virgin green valleys,
the birds towards the evening singing on every tree,
the stags that came tamely to the water as to a master's whistle
and the fresh air from the east
and the glisten of gold stones in the sunlight.

Fifteen days later we sighted Guiana, to our great joy,
and a strong push of northerly wind blew that afternoon
and by night we reached a place where the river opens into three branches
and that night we lay at anchor under the stars, smelling the fragance of
    Guiana.
The nearness of the land of Guiana!
But we had to head back eastward
because the rains began: those great downpours
and the rivers flooded, and endless swamps—
leaving behind Guiana with its sword of fire,
leaving Guiana to the sun, whom they worship.
And we entered the sea once more, all very sad...

Las mujeres nos quedaban mirando

. . . Y una tarde llegamos a una ciudad en mitad de un valle
rodeada de árboles frutales,
de habitantes tan quietos que no se oye ningún ruido ni tumulto,
ni riñen nunca, ni gritan, sino que se hablan en voz baja unos a otros,
que parece que nadie la habitara.
Suelen salir de noche a cantar bajo la luna
y bailar al son de sus instrumentos de viento,
y frecuentemente nos pedían que cantáramos y bailáramos con ellos,
y a veces lo hacíamos,
y reían muy alegres y parecía
que querían comprender las palabras de los cantos.
Las mujeres nos quedaban mirando,
y algunas se acercaron a preguntarnos
si las mujeres de nuestra tierra son también del color de nosotros.

The Women Kept Looking at Us

. . . And one afternoon we came to a town surrounded by fruit trees
in the middle of a valley,
inhabited by people so peaceful that never a noise or commotion is heard,
nor do they ever quarrel, or yell, but speak in a low voice to one another,
making it seem as if nobody lived there.
They usually go out at night to sing in the moonlight
and dance as they play their wind instruments,
and they often requested that we sing and dance with them,
and sometimes we would do so,
and they'd laugh in high spirits and it seemed
that they wanted to understand the words of our songs.
The women kept looking at us,
and some came up to ask us
if the women in our country also had skin the color of ours.

Omagua

Por las grandes cosas que dijo haber visto el Capitán Orellana!
Por las grandes cosas que dijo haber visto el Capitán Orellana!
Decían tantas cosas del Río y las provincias a él comarcanas
y especialmente la provincia de Omagua,
        que fuimos en busca de Omagua,
por aquella tierra llana que hay casi hasta el mar
parando todos los días a la hora de vísperas
y los hombres bajando a tierra a pescar y mariscquear.
Y dos hombres salieron a buscar comida juntos
y nunca más volvieron.
Nunca se supo qué se hicieron.
Muchos indios venían en canoas por el río
y les preguntaban a gritos por Omagua.
¡Omagua! ¡Omagua!
Orsúa decía:
que encanecerían buscando la tierra los que salieron muchachos.
Los hombres se morían de hambre en aquel gran desierto de agua.
Y ya llevábamos más de 700 leguas sin ver Omagua.
¡Omagua! ¡Omagua!
¡Oh esperanzas de la tierra de Omagua!

Y una noche en el pueblo de casas redondas y grandes
cubiertas de hojas de palma hasta el suelo,
días antes que mataran a Orsúa entre las ollas de comida,
paseándose Núñez de Guevara por el calor que hacía,
vio pasar por la empalizada una sombra y dijo:
"¡Pedro de Orsúa, Governador del Dorado y Omagua,
Dios te perdone!"
Y dijo que corrió tras el bulto en la oscuridad
y no era nadie.

Omagua

For the grand things Captain Orellana said he had seen!
For the grand things Captain Orellana said he had seen!
They used to say so many things about the River and the provinces bordering it,
especially the province of Omagua.
                And so we went off in search of Omagua,
along that flat country which verges on the sea,
halting every day at the hour of vespers
and the men would go ashore to fish and gather shellfish.
And two men went out to hunt for food together
and never made it back.
We never found out what became of them.
Many Indians used to come in canoes along the river
and they were questioned with shouts about Omagua.
Omagua! Omagua!
Orsúa used to say:
those who set out young lads would grow grey-haired searching for the land.
Men were dying of hunger in that great wilderness of water.
And in time we traveled more than 700 leagues without seeing Omagua.
Omagua! Omagua!
Oh the hopes that land of Omagua raised!

And one night in a village of big round houses
thatched with palm leaves down to the ground,
a few days before they would kill Orsúa among the mess kettles,
Núñez de Guevara was out walking for relief from the heat
when he saw a shadow passing by the palisade that said:
"Pedro de Orsúa, Governor of El Dorado and Omagua,
may God forgive thee!"
And he said he chased after the form in the dark
and that it was no one.

John Roach, marinero

De su bajada en Sur América a cortar leña
y su cautiverio en una tribu errante de Indios.

...Estos indios son llamados Wolaways, o cabezas chatas,
y deben su nombre a la forma de sus cabezas.
Sus cuerpos son de color de tierra y los pintan como tinajas
y se visten con grandes plumajes como pájaros.
No tienen residencia fija sino que andan corriendo en el bosque
y si el viento de la noche o las animales mueven las hojas
se levantan y corren tal vez toda esa noche
y no tienen medios para contar el tiempo
y su vida es sin años.

John Roach, Mariner

From his stop in South America to cut firewood
and his captivity among a wandering tribe of Indians.

. . . These Indians are called Wolaways, or flat heads,
and owe their name to the shape of their heads.
Their bodies are earth-colored and they paint them like clay jugs
and wear great plumes like birds.
They have no fixed dwelling place but roam around in the woods
and if some night the wind or the animals move the leaves
they pick themselves up and run perhaps all that night
and they possess no ways for telling time
and years aren't part of their life.

Estrella encontrada muerta en Park Avenue

Me despertaron los rayos
como un ruido de mudanzas y de rodar de muebles en un piso de arriba
y después como millones de radios
o de trenes subterráneos
o aviones de bombardeo
y parecía que venían todos los rayos del mundo
a los pararrayos de los rascacielos de Nueva York
y corrían desde la Catedral de St. John the Divine hasta el edificio del Times
      No nos hables Tú. No nos hables Tú que moriremos
desde la torre de Woolworth hasta el edificio del Chrysler
y los relámpagos iluminando los rascacielos como fotógrafos
      Que nos hable Moisés.
      No nos hables Tú que moriremos
"Debe haber muerto anoche como a las 3 a.m."
dijo después el New York Times.
Yo estaba despierto entonces. Me despertaron los rayos.
El cielo constelado de apartamentos y de baños
las luces de legítimos e ilegítimos amores
y de los que rezan, o roban allá arriba una caja de hierro
o violan a una muchacha con un radio a todo volumen
o se masturban, o no pueden dormir
y los que se están desvistiendo (y sus cortinas que se corren)
Y el ruido de los Elevados de la 3ª Avenida
y los trenes que en la Calle 125 salen de la tierra
y nuevamente se hunden,
un autobús parándose y acelerando en una esquina
(bajo la lluvia), el grito, tal vez, de una mujer en el parque,

Star Found Dead on Park Avenue

The bolts of lightning woke me up
like the noise of furniture being moved and rolled across a floor upstairs
and later like millions of radios
or subway trains
or bombers
and it seemed that all the thunderbolts in the world
were hitting the lightning rods of skyscrapers in New York
and they stretched from the Cathedral of St. John the Divine to the Times
    building
        Speak not to us, Lord. Speak not to us lest we die
from the Woolworth Tower to the Chrysler Building
and the flashes were lighting up the skyscrapers like photographers
        Let Moses speak to us.
        Speak not to us, Lord, lest we die
"He probably died last night around 3 a.m."
the New York Times later said.
I was awake then. The lightning woke me up.
The sky made starry by apartments and bathrooms
the lights of lawful and illicit love affairs
and of people praying, or robbing a safe right upstairs
or raping a girl as a radio plays full blast
or masturbating, or not being able to sleep
and people getting undressed (and drawing their curtains)
And the noise from the 3rd Avenue El
and the trains that come out of the ground at 125th Street
and go back down again,
a bus stopping and starting up at a corner
(in the rain), the scream, perhaps, of a woman in the park,

y el alarido de las ambulancias en las calles desiertas
o los rojos bomberos que no sabemos si corren al número nuestro
"...Su cuerpo fue encontrado por Max Hilton, el artista,
que dijo a la policía lo encontró en el piso del baño,
el dibujo del piso grabado en su mejilla mojada
y apretando aún en su mano un frasco de píldoras blancas,
y en el aposento un radio sonando a todo volumen
sin ninguna estación."

and the wailing of ambulances in the empty streets
or the red fire engines for all we know speeding to our own address
". . . His body was found by Max Hilton, the artist,
who told police he found him on the bathroom floor,
the floor's pattern pressed into his wet cheek
and he was still clutching a vial of white pills in his hand,
and in the bedroom a radio was playing full blast
no station at all."

Back in Nicaragua

Con Walker en Nicaragua

En una cabaña solitaria en la frontera,
yo, Clinton Rollins, sin pretensión literaria,
me entretengo en escribir mis memorias.
Y mis pensamientos de viejo retroceden:

Las cosas que hace cincuenta años sucedieron...

Hispanoamericanos que he conocido
        —a los que he aprendido a querer...
Y aquel olor tibio, dulzón, verde, de Centro América.
Las casas blancas con tejas rojas y con grandes aleros llenas de sol,
y un patio tropical con una fuente y una mujer junto a la fuente.
Y el calor que hacía crecer más nuestras barbas.
¡Las escenas que hoy vuelven a mi memoria!
Una ola gris que viene borrando los montes
y un sordo rumor de inundación recorriendo la selva
y los aullidos de los monos en la margen opuesta
y después las gotas de gruesos metálicos golpes en los techos de zinc
y corren a quitar la ropa en las barandas de las haciendas
y después la ola gris y el sordo rumor alejándose
y otra vez el silencio...
Y cómo olía a maleza y el río se coloreaba de clorofila,
y el vaporcito se divisaba allá, tranquilo,
anclado a la sombra de la selva.
Y el repentino planazo de la iguana en el agua,
el estruendo de los troncos cayendo,
el disparo distante de un rifle,
una palabra en español que gritan lejos,
la risa de las negras lavando la ropa
y un canto caribe.

With Walker in Nicaragua

In a lonely cabin on the frontier,
I, Clinton Rollins, attempting no literary style,
pass the time by penning my memories.
And as an old man my thoughts wander back:

The things that happened fifty years ago . . .

Spanish-Americans I have known
        —whom I have grown to like . . .
And that warm, sweet, green odor of Central America.
The white houses with red-tiled roofs and with wide sunny eaves,
and a tropical courtyard with a fountain and a woman by the fountain.
And the heat making our beards grow longer.
What scenes return to my memory now!
A grey wave that comes blotting out the hills
and a muffled sound of flood waters rushing through the jungle
and the howls of monkeys on the opposite bank
and then the heavy, metallic beating of raindrops on the tin roofs
and the people running to take in the clothes from the ranch porches
and later the grey wave and the muffled sound moving off
and once again the silence . . .
And how it smelled of underbrush and the river turned leaf-green,
how the little steamboat looked there, calm as could be,
anchored to the shade of the jungle.
And the sudden flop of an iguana into the water,
the rumble of falling timber,
the distant shot of a rifle,
a Spanish word shouted from afar,
the laughter of the black women washing clothes
and a Caribbean song.

Mis compañeros en aquella expedición con William Walker:
Aquiles Kewen, el aristócrata, que cayó peleando en Rivas;
Chris Lily, el boxeador,
degollado borracho una noche junto a una brillante laguna;
William Stocker (Bill), con su cara de pirata—y buen muchacho—
que se casó allá despés y vivía junto al lago de Managua
(y yo comí una vez en su casa);
y Crocker, el afeminado,
que murió jadeante en Rivas,
con su sucia barba rubia pesada de sangre,
y un brazo colgándole y en el otro a medio descargar el revólver;
Skelter, el petulante, que murió del cólera;
y Dixie, vendedor de periódicos, —el corneta—
que mejor que las gaitas escocesas en Lucknow,
la noche que el coronel Jack rompió las líneas,
tocó esa corneta.
De Brissot, Dolan, Henry, Bob Gray;
el bandido, el desilusionado, el vago, el buscador de tesoros;
los que quedaron colgados de los árboles y meciéndose
bajo los hediondos cóndores negros y la luna
o tendidos en los llanos con un coyote-solo y la luna,
el rifle junto a ellos;
o en las calientes calles empedradas llenas de gritos,
o blancos como conchas en la costa
donde las mareas los están siempre cubriendo y descubriendo.
Los que pasaron todos esos peligros y aún viven todavía.
Los que se quedaron para casarse allá después
y vivir en paz en esa tierra
y estarán esta tarde sentados recordando
(pensando escribir tal vez un día sus memorias),
y su esposa que es de esa tierra, y los nietos jugando...
Los que desertaron con Turley, adentro, hacia las minas de oro
y fueron rodeados por nativos y perecieron.
El hombre que cayó dormido al agua desde un barco
—soñando tal vez con batallas—
y nadie oyó sus gritos en la oscuridad

My companions on that expedition with William Walker:
Achilles Kewen, the aristocrat, who fell fighting at Rivas;
Chris Lilly, the boxer,
his throat cut while drunk one night beside a shining lagoon;
William Stoker (Bill), with his pirate's face—and a good man—
who got married there afterwards and lived by Lake Managua
(and I ate once at his house);
and Crocker, the pretty-boy,
who died gasping for breath at Rivas,
with his dirty, blond beard heavy with blood,
and one arm dangling and a half-empty revolver in the other;
Skelter, the braggart, who died of cholera;
and Dixie, the newsboy—the bugler—
who on the night Colonel Jack broke through the lines
was better than the Scottish bagpipes at Lucknow
playing his bugle.
De Brissot, Dolan, Henry, Bob Gray;
the bandit, the doubting Thomas, the bum, the treasure hunter;
the ones who were hanged from trees and left swinging
beneath the stinking black vultures and the moon
or sprawled on the plains with a lone coyote and the moon,
their rifle beside them;
or in the hot, cobbled streets filled with shouts,
or white like shells on the seashore
where the tides are always covering and uncovering them.
The ones who survived all those dangers and are even still alive.
The ones who stayed there afterwards to get married
and to live in peace in that land
and who this afternoon probably sit remembering
(thinking about how one day they might pen their memories),
and their wife who is from that land, and their grandchildren playing . . .
The ones who deserted with Turley, inland, toward the gold mines
and were surrounded by natives and perished.
The man who while sleeping fell from a boat into the water
—dreaming perhaps of battles—
and not a soul heard his cries in the darkness,

si es que gritó.
Los que fueron fusilados por Walker contra una iglesia gris.
        Y después, el propio Walker, fusilado...

Hornsby había estado en Nicaragua
y hablaba de sus lagos azules entre montes azules bajo el cielo azul,
y que era la ruta del Tránsito y la gran vía,
el muelle de América,
y que se llenaría de barcos mercantes y de extranjeros
hablando todas las lenguas, esperando el Canal;
y cada barco trayendo nuevos aventureros;
y las verdes plantaciones con sus grandes casas blancas con terrazas;
y la esposa del plantador instruyendo a los hijos de los negros;
y los campos con aserríos y avenidas de palmeras y rumores de ingenios
y los caminos llenos de diligencias azules
y las tucas bajando los ríos.

Vi por primera vez a Walker en San Francisco:
recuerdo como si lo viera su rostro rubio como el de un tigre;
sus ojos grises, sin pupilas, fijos como los de un ciego,
pero que se dilataban y se encendían como pólvora en los combates,
y su piel de pecas borrosas, su palidez, sus modales de clérigo,
su voz, descolorida como sus ojos, fría y afilada,
en una boca sin labios.
Y la voz de una mujer no era más suave que la suya:
la de los serenos anuncios de las sentencias de muerte...
La que arrastró a tantos a la boca de la muerte en los combates.
Nunca bebía ni fumaba y no llevaba uniforme.
Ninguno fue su amigo.
Y no recuerdo haberlo visto jamás sonreír.

Zarpamos de San Francisco el 55.
Aquiles Kewen y Bill y Crocker, Hornsby y los demás:
        —a bordo de un buque filibustero!
Hubo tormentas en Tehuantepec, y por las noches
volcanes intermitentes en la costa como faros.

if he did cry out.
The ones who were shot by Walker against a grey church.
        And later, Walker himself, shot . . .

Hornsby had been in Nicaragua
and he spoke of its blue lakes amid blue mountains under a blue sky,
and how it was the Transit route and the great passageway,
the pier of America,
and how it would teem with merchant ships and with foreigners
speaking all tongues, waiting for the Canal;
and each ship bringing new adventurers,
and the green plantations with their great white houses with verandas;
and the planter's wife instructing the children of the blacks;
and the countryside with sawmills and palm-lined avenues humming with
    sugar mills
and the roads filled with blue stagecoaches
and the logs floating down the rivers.

I saw Walker for the first time in San Francisco:
I remember him as if I were seeing his blond face like a tiger's;
his grey eyes, without pupils, fixed like a blind man's,
but which expanded and flashed like gunpowder in combat,
and his skin faintly freckled, his paleness, his clergyman's ways,
his voice, colorless like his eyes, cold and sharp,
in a mouth without lips.
And a woman's voice was hardly softer than his:
that calm voice of his announcing death sentences . . .
that swept so many into the jaws of death in combat.
He never drank or smoked and he wore no uniform.
Nobody was his friend.
And I don't remember ever having seen him smile.

We set sail from San Francisco in '55.
Achilles Kewen and Bill and Crocker, Hornsby and the others:
        —on board a filibuster brig!
There were storms in Tehuantepec, and during the nights
volcanos every now and then along the coast like beacons.

En el Golfo de Fonseca, tras las islas azules,
viejos volcanes ruinosos como pirámides,
parecían mirarnos:
¡La tierra donde pasaríamos tantas aventuras,
donde tantos de nosotros morirían de peste o peleando!
Y la selva con un silbido llamando, llamando,
con sus gruesas hojas carnosas, rotas, chorreando agua;
y como un constante quejido...
Y nadie nos había hecho daño, y traíamos la guerra.

Cuando vimos por primera vez el lago de Nicaragua
al llegar la vanguardia a una vuelta del camino,
hicimos alto, con una sola exclamación:
                    —Ometepe!
El liso lago azul y la Isla
con sus dos volcanes gemelos como pechos
unidos al nivel del agua por sus bases,
que parecía que se hundían en el agua,
y el humo humilde de sus aldeas levantándose.
Y por la transparencia del aire
                    parecían cerca.
Y abajo la arena vidriosa, y a lo lejos
las torres de la iglesia de Rivas.

Y Rivas después y los primeros disparos,
Walker delante a caballo como una bandera,
y era mediodía y nos pesaba la ropa con el sol.
Y Kewen y Crocker fueron heridos.
¡*Fuego!* gritó Kewen
y corrimos por la calle gris amurallada,
Crocker con el revólver plateado gritando.
Rivas quedó llena de gritos y de sangre y de incendios bajo el sol
y volvimos al puerto azul entre colinas
con sus curvos cocos amarillos cabeceándose
y la pequeña embarcación costarricense en la bahía.
Hubo grandes vientos esa noche

In the Gulf of Fonseca, behind blue islands,
crumbling old volcanos like pyramids
seemed to be watching us:
The land where we would go through so many adventures,
where so many of us would die by fever or fighting!
And the jungle with a whistle calling, calling,
with its thick leaves like flesh, rattan palms, rushing water;
and like a constant moan . . .
No one had done us any harm, and we brought war.

When we saw Lake Nicaragua for the first time,
upon reaching the front at a bend in the road,
we halted, with a single exclamation:
                    —Ometepe!
The smooth blue lake and the Island
with its two twin volcanos like breasts
joined at water level by their bases,
which looked like they were sinking in the water,
and the humble smoke rising from its villages.
And through the air's clearness
                    they seemed close by.
And beneath us that glassy sand, and in the distance
the steeples of the church at Rivas.

So Rivas next and the first shots,
Walker in front on horseback like a flag.
It was noonday, and our sun-drenched clothes felt heavy on us.
Then Kewen and Crocker were wounded.
Fire! shouted Kewen
and we ran through the grey, walled street,
Crocker with his silver-plated revolver shouting.
Rivas was left filled with shouts and blood and fires burning in the sun's glare
and we returned to that blue port nestled in hills
with their curved yellow coconut palms swaying
and a small Costa Rican ship in the harbor.
There were high winds that night

con la luna veloz entre nubes plateadas y negras.
—Y De Brissot en su camilla rencoroso con Walker...

Y en León las noches eran frescas
con guitarras distantes bajo balcones de hierro
y el viento mecía los faroles dorados frente a las casas.
Y al acercarnos a la ciudad
se oía a lo lejos los centinelas paseándose
y un "alerta" sucesivo corriendo de calle en calle.
Las voces de las gentes nos parecían extrañas
y sus palabras terminaban con languidez como en un canto.
Y el grito del centinela era tan musical como el de un pájaro en la tarde.
Como en las aldeas chorreadas de nieve de los Estados Unidos
se oyen las voces de los centinelas en la tarde
alegres, largas y claras.
Y el grito de "alerta" resonaba de nuevo.
                    Las muchachas de Nicaragua
llevaban rosarios colgados con cruces de oro
y sartas de perlas en la frente y trenzas negras.
Y nos enamoramos de las mujeres de esa tierra.

Un día nos embarcamos en La Virgen, hacia Granada,
frente a los dos volcanes callados como dos guardas azules.
El lago estaba inmóvil
y ya las garzas volaban por todas partes sobre el lago
como grandes flores blancas, hacia las islas donde duermen,
y las bandadas de patos chillones iban en busca de refugio.
Apagamos en la noche el motor tembloroso frente a Granada,
y sólo se oían las olas contra el barco.

with the moon swift among the silvery dark clouds.
—And De Brissot in a hospital bed, angry at Walker...

And in León the nights were cool
with distant guitars below wrought-iron balconies
and the wind swinging the golden lamps in front of the houses.
And as we neared the city
we heard from afar the sentries pacing back and forth
and an "alerta" one after the other running from street to street.
The voices of the people sounded strange to us
and their words ended faintly as in a song.
And the sentry's cry was as musical as a bird's in the evening.
Just the way in snow-covered small towns in the States,
come evening one hears the watchmen's voices
cheery, full and clear.
And the cry of "alerta" resounded once more.
                    The girls in Nicaragua
wore rosaries with gold crosses hanging from them
and strings of pearls around their heads and black tresses.
And we fell in love with the women of that land.

One day we embarked on the *Virgen,* for Granada,
in front of those two silent volcanos like two blue guards.
The lake was glassy smooth
and all at once herons everywhere flew over the lake
as if great white flowers, toward islands where they sleep,
and flocks of screaming ducks took off in search of shelter.
At night we stopped the trembling engine in front of Granada,
and only the waves against the boat could be heard.

Cubrimos con lona nuestras luces,
echamos el ancla con sigilo,
atamos un cable a un árbol de la costa,
y bajando los botes, desembarcamos.
Avanzamos invisibles en la oscuridad con nuestros uniformes negros
　　　—la oscuridad llena de luciérnagas y grillos—
oyendo cada leve rumor como un gran ruido.
Y cuando sonó la alarma en las espesas torres ya fue tarde,
y el alba se alzó de pronto de las aguas alumbrando
las extrañas calles, serias y vacías
de la ciudad tomada:
con los filibusteros de uniforme negro en las esquinas
y la bandera de la Estrella Roja en San Francisco.

Y después hubo paz.
Walker habló de paz y Conciliación Nacional
y juró de rodillas la Constitución con Corral en la iglesia.

Granada despertaba cada mañana con campanas
y pregones de vendedoras en las calles:
　　　　Tengo naranjas, papayas, jocotes,
　　　　melones de agua, de oro, zapotes,
　　　　　　¿quieren comprar?
y vendedores de agua con sus pipas gritando:
　　　　¡Aaaaaaaagua, aaaagua, aaaagua!
Todo el día refrescaba las calles ese grito de agua
y había ventas de refrescos de colores en las calles
—unas ventas que allá llaman caramancheles—
y procesiones de muchachas venían del lago con sus cántaros
y en el lago las lavanderas semidesnudas lavaban cantando,
y los hombres dando de beber o bañando a sus caballos.
Y se oía cantar la *Salve Regina* por las tardes
y el aire era entonces tan puro que se oían
todas las conversaciones de las gentes en sus puertas
y las serenatas claras desde lejos;
y de noche cantaban en el patio las húmedas ranas,

We covered our lanterns with canvas,
dropped anchor stealthily,
attached a cable to a tree on the shore,
and lowering some launches, we disembarked.
No one could see us advancing in the darkness with our black uniforms
      —the darkness full of fireflies and crickets—
hearing every little noise as if a big racket.
And by the time the alarm was sounded in the thick towers it was late,
as the dawn suddenly rose from the waters lighting
the foreign streets, grave and empty
of the captured town:
with filibusters in black uniform on the streetcorners
and our flag with its Red Star at St. Francis.

And then there was peace.
Walker spoke of peace and National Reconciliation
and kneeling with Corral in church he swore to observe the Constitution.

Granada would awake each morning with bells
and cries of vendors in the streets:
        I have oranges, papayas, jocotes,
        watermelons, musk melons, zapotes!
           —Who wants to buy?
and water vendors with their casks crying out:
        Waaaaaaaater, waaaater, waaaater!
All day long that cry of water would cool the streets
and there were stands with drinks of all colors in the streets
—some stands they call canteens there—
and processions of girls would come from the lake with their jars
and in the lake half-naked washerwomen washed laundry singing,
while men would be watering or bathing their horses.
And you'd hear the *Salve Regina* being sung through the evenings
and the air was so pure then you could hear
all the conversations of people in their doorways
and the clear serenades from afar;
and at night wet frogs used to sing in the courtyard,

o la voz de una joven tras las tapias,
y nos acostábamos oyendo el chorrear de las tejas de barro en el húmedo patio
y se nos iban confundiendo las ideas
y las largas hileras de faroles se extinguían poco a poco,
hasta otro día con campanas otra vez y los gritos de agua.

Walker de buen humor daba largas cabalgatas por las calles.
—Pero Corral cabizbajo no salía de su casa...
Y aquel día en que fue preso (juzgado por el Consejo de Guerra,
y el reo encomendado a la clemencia de Walker,
y Walker: que el reo sería fusilado a las doce del día)
vinieron señoras, con la madre, y las tres hijas llorando,
las dos menores abrazadas a las rodillas de Walker;
y él: en medio de sus oficiales y rodeado de la guardia cubana.
Y los filibusteros afuera oíamos en silencio.
Y aquel hombre que había tenido una novia en Nashville,
Helen Martin, sordomuda,
                    que murió de fiebre amarilla,
—por la cual aprendió el lenguaje de manos
y trazaban entre ellos signos silenciosos en el aire—,
como si una compasión fugaz como el vuelo de un párpado
hubiera cruzado entonces sus incoloros ojos de hielo,
dijo levantando la mano:
                    —que Corral no sería fusilado
a las doce del día... sino a las dos de la tarde.
Y afuera nosotros, los filibusteros,
                    estábamos pendientes.
Y vimos la plaza ensombrecerse bajo una nube,
las palmeras quietas, la Catedral, la gran cruz de piedra,
y al fin de la Calzada, como un muro, el lago plomo.
Y un soldado entonces: —¡Qué generoso!
                    "God, how generous!"
riendo a carcajadas;
y hubo que empujarlo para que él no lo oyera.
Corral fue fusilado a las dos de la tarde.

or a young woman's voice behind adobe walls,
and we went to bed listening to the trickle from the clay tiles in the wet
    courtyard
and our thoughts would be getting mixed up
and the long rows of street lamps were put out one after the other,
until the next day with bells again and the cries of water.

Walker in good spirits produced long cavalcades through the streets.
—But, downhearted, Corral never left his house...
And that day on which he was arrested (tried by court-martial,
the prisoner then threw himself on the mercy of Walker,
and Walker: that the prisoner would be shot at noon)
ladies came, with Señora Corral, and her three daughters weeping,
the youngest two embracing Walker's knees;
and he: in between officers and surrounded by his Cuban bodyguards.
An we filibusters outside listened in silence.
And that man who'd had a sweetheart in Nashville,
Helen Martin, a deaf-mute,
                        who died of yellow fever,
—for whom he learned the language of hands
and together they'd make silent signs in the air—
as if a fleeting compassion like the batting of an eyelid
had then crossed his colorless eyes of ice,
lifting his hand he said:
                        —that Corral would not be shot
at noon...but at two in the afternoon.
And outside we, the filibusters,
                        were hung in doubt.
And we saw the town square overshadowed by a cloud,
the still palm trees, the Cathedral, the great stone cross,
and at the end of Main Street, like a wall, the leaden lake.
And a soldier then: "Good God, how generous!"
bursting into a loud guffaw;
and he had to be taken off so he wouldn't be heard.
Corral was shot at two in the afternoon.

Geelman dio la orden:
Walker a cierta distancia, a caballo, sin tomar parte.
Y hubo luto en muchas casas. Oímos esos llantos.
Y después hubo una gran calma, como antes de una tempestad.

Walker se proclamó Presidente
y decretó la esclavitud y la confiscación de bienes.
Y enemigos que no veíamos alrededor de lagunas se juntaban.

La peste hizo su entrada con tambores fúnebres ese invierno.
Todo estaba tranquilo un día,
cuando empezaron a oírse las primeras descargas acercándose
y los gritos de vivas en las afueras,
y el ruido de las armas y las balas de los rifles
cada vez más cerca,
y el enemigo dirigiéndose con rapidez en dirección a la plaza.
—A mí me habían dejado en Granada y puedo contarlo.
Los hombres desarmados en sus casas y matados delante de sus familias;
y un niño asesinado mientras estaba comiendo.
Cortada la comunicación con el muelle.
—Sitiados.
        Las patrullas abajo golpeando las puertas.
Y del enemigo llegaban risas y guitarras con fogatas por la noche.
Y al amanecer, había mujeres enlutadas en las calles.
Y entonces vino aquel inglés C. F. Henningsen,
que había peleado contra el Zar y en España y por la independencia de Hungría.
¡Y si hubiéramos podido entonces embarcarnos
y dejar la desolada Granada
        —el Castillo Blanco, como nosotros le decíamos—
con sus calles ensangrentadas y sus pozos hediondos llenos de muertos,
y las muecas de los muertos a la luz de los incendios en las calles!
Nos defendíamos de las balas tras montones de muertos.
El día era caliente, y el aire lleno de humo de los incendios.
Y hora tras hora sin dejar de mirarlos,
        sin dejar de mirar a los enemigos,

Gilman gave the order:
Walker some distance away, on horseback, not taking part.
There was mourning in many houses. We heard the weeping.
And afterward there was a great calm, like the calm before a storm.

Walker proclaimed himself President
and he decreed slavery and the seizure of estates.
Meantime enemy troops we didn't see were mustering around lagoons.

The plague made its entrance with funeral drums that winter.
All was peaceful one day,
when the first volleys began to be heard drawing near
and the loud vivas on the outskirts,
and the noise of weapons and the bullets from rifles
nearer and nearer,
and the enemy moving fast in the direction of the main square.
—They'd left me behind in Granada, so I can tell the story.
Unarmed men in their homes killed in front of their families;
and a little boy murdered while eating his dinner.
Communication with the pier was cut.
—Besieged.
   Patrols downstairs banging on the doors.
And from the enemy boomed laughter and guitars with bonfires during the
  night.
And at daybreak, there were women grief-striken in the streets.
And then came that Englishman, C. F. Henningsen,
who'd fought against the Czar and in Spain and for the independence of
  Hungary.
If only we could have sailed off right then
and left that ruined Granada
   —*the White Castle,* as we used to call it—
with its bloodstained streets and its stinking wells full of corpses,
and the dead's grimaces lit by fires in the streets!
We protected ourselves from bullets behind piles of corpses.
Day was hot, and the air full of smoke from the fires.
And hour after hour without failing to see them,
   without failing to see enemy troops,

hasta que por fin vino la noche
    y se callaron los rifles.
Henningsen hizo trincheras esa noche.
Y al día siguiente
el sol iba saliendo del lago como una isla de oro
y los disparos y el silbido de las balas y las quejas
nos anunciaron que un día más de horror había llegado.
Y habíamos venido a una tierra extraña en busca de oro
y allí estaba el humo negro por todas partes
y las calles llenas de mercancías y de muertos.
Sólo se oyeron disparos a distancia el resto del día
y los lamentos de los atacados por el cólera,
y la voz serena de Henningsen animando.
En los balcones en los que antes se sentaran las muchachas
con sus ayas,
ahora asomaban con sus largos rifles,
                    los rifleros,
y en vez de polkas y valses, los disparos.
Al otro día
las últimas casas de la plaza fueron quemadas.
La ciudad con las descargas y el humo y la pólvora parecía de lejos
como en un día de fiesta!

La estación de las lluvias había cesado
y la fiebre se propagaba como un incendio.
Nos echaban de noche los muertos del cólera en el agua
y se oían los gritos de los enfermos que deliraban pidiendo agua
                    —¡Agua, agua!
Arrojábamos los cadáveres a los incendios
y el humo acre que despedían nos enrojecía los ojos
y ese humo
y el polvo
y el sol sobre el empedrado y las llamas de las casas y la pólvora
secaban más nuestras bocas
y los soldados dejaban de pelear para toser
y eran heridos mientras tosían

until night finally came
        and the rifles quieted down.
Henningsen dug trenches that night.
And the following day
the sun rose up out of the lake like an island of gold
and the shots and the whistling of bullets and the groans
let us know one more day of horror had arrived.
And we'd come to a foreign land in search of gold
and there black smoke was everywhere
and streets filled with shop goods and corpses.
All that could be heard the rest of the day were shots
and the moans of those hit by cholera,
and the calm voice of Henningsen giving encouragement.
In balconies where before girls might have been sitting
with their governesses,
now riflemen could be seen,
                with their long rifles,
and instead of polkas and waltzes, gunfire.
By the next day
the last houses on the square were burned down.
From afar the town with shooting and smoke and fireworks
looked the way it does on a holiday!

The rainy season had ended
and the fever was spreading like a fire.
At night we dumped those dead from cholera into the water
and cries could be heard from the sick who were delirious begging for water
                —Water, water!
We threw the corpses into fires
and the acrid smoke they gave off made our eyes red
and that smoke
and the dust
and the sun on the pavement and the flames from the houses and the
    gunpowder
dried our mouths more
and soldiers stopped fighting to cough
and were wounded while they coughed

y caían por tierra todavía tosiendo.
Se hacían nuevos intentos por llegar al lago
que brillaba al final de la calle como vidrio,
                    blanco como hielo.
Sabíamos que muchos cuerpos se quemaban.
Y muchas quejas subían de las calles por la noche.
Y de las afueras, el olor dulzón de los muertos.
Y Walker entretanto:
        ¡tomando baños de mar en San Juan del Sur!
Adonde no llegan las detonaciones de los cañones
y aun tal vez ni nuestros mensajes.

Los días pasaban sin recibir ninguna noticia.
Y vuelvo a ver aún ahora en mis pesadillas nocturnas esos días.

Ya no se reconocían las casas que habían sido familiares
y apenas si se distinguían las calles bajo los escombros:
        —una imagen de la Virgen colgada sola en el muro negro.
Y el lago de color de ceniza tras los escombros.
        Agua del color de los ojos de Walker
tras los escombros
que formaban siluetas irregulares por la noche.
Y recuerdo una iglesia de la que no quedaba sino el pórtico
como un arco de triunfo.

Y al reguero de pólvora en la calle del lago se le dio fuego.
Y el mensaje de Henningsen fue:
"Su orden fue obedicida, señor:
        Granada ha dejado de existir."

and dropped to the ground still coughing.
New plans were made to reach the lake
which shined at the end of the street like glass,
                              white as ice.
We knew that many bodies were being burned.
And many groans rose from the streets during the night.
And from the outskirts, the sweet odor of the dead.
And Walker meanwhile:
                taking dips in the ocean at San Juan del Sur!
Where the blasts from the cannons did not reach
nor perhaps even our messages.

The days went by without receiving any news.
And I still relive those days in my dark nightmares.

Houses that had been familiar were no longer recognizable
and the streets could hardly be distinguished beneath the rubble:
                —a statue of the Virgin hanging by itself on a black wall.
And the ash-colored lake behind the rubble.
                Water the color of Walker's eyes
behind the rubble
which formed odd silhouettes during the night.
And I remember a church with nothing left standing but the portico
like a triumphal arch.

And those flames spread like wildfire in the street from the lake.
And Henningsen's message was:
"Your order has been obeyed, sir:
                Granada is no more."

Por fin llegó el auxilio,
con Walker en persona que se quedó en el barco,
y reconocimos en la noche los disparos desde lejos.
El agua estaba quieta y pesada como el acero
y los fogonazos de los rifles se reflejaban como relámpagos.
Y entonces fue cuando aquel coronel Jack, de Kentucky,
rompió las líneas,
y cuando Dixie, el vendedor de periódicos, tocó la corneta
y en la oscuridad de la noche de colina en colina
brilló como una luminaria esa corneta
hasta llegar hasta nosotros los sitiados,
haciendo de los 350 que venían
como un ejército inmenso en perfectas formaciones avanzando
echándose a tierra todos a una
y poniéndose de pie y disparando con los largos rifles.
Eran cerca de las 2 de la madrugada del 14
cuando todo estuvo a bordo.
Henningsen fue el último en dejar Granada.
Entró a la gran plaza desolada
y allí vio a su alrededor la obra que había hecho;
levantó un carbón
y escribió en un cuero chamuscado el epitafio:

> AQUI FUE GRANADA
> "HERE WAS GRANADA"

lo clavó con una lanza en mitad de la plaza,
y se fue.

Amaban a Granada como a una mujer.
Todavía asoman las lágrimas a sus ojos
cuando recuerdan la pérdida de su querida Granada
la ciudad de los Chamorros...
> Donde una vez hubo amor.

Help finally arrived,
with Walker himself, who stayed on the boat,
and we could make out the shots in the night from afar.
The water was still and heavy like steel
and the flashes from the rifles reflected like lightning.
And it was then that Colonel Jack, from Kentucky,
broke through the lines,
as Dixie, the newsboy, played his bugle
and in the darkness of midnight from hill to hill
that bugle shined like a glorious light
coming up to us beleaguered souls,
making the 350 who came
act like an immense army in perfect formations advancing
hitting the dirt all as one
and getting up, with their long rifles
                    firing.
It was nearly two in the morning on the 14th
when all were on board.
Henningsen was the last to leave Granada.
He went into the ruined main square
and there saw around him the work that had been done;
he picked up a dead ember
and wrote on a piece of scorched hide the epitaph:

            "HERE WAS GRANADA"

then stuck it up on a lance in the middle of the square,
and so it was.

They loved Granada like a woman.
Even today tears well up in their eyes
when they remember the loss of their dear Granada
the town of the Chamorros...
            Where once there was love.

¡Al fin las aguas limpias,
las limpias brisas azules de la madrugada
y fuera de Granada con sus muertos rojos y teas
y ayes y estertores y gritos y estampidos
y el olor de las casas, trapos, muebles, basuras, cadáveres que se queman!
Hacia los dos volcanes hermanos
que se levantan de las aguas,
y a través de las aldeas cerradas
          con los perros ladrando. . .
Y los hombres volvieron a los Estados Unidos.

Yo me quedé un tiempo en el país, viviendo en León.
Y Bill Deshon, Shipley, Dixie, Bob Gray, Bill Stocker,
y otros, llegaron a verme
y me contaron lo de la segunda expedición
                y la muerte de Walker.

Que levó anclas silenciosamente una noche en el Mississippi:
Desembarcaron en la costa de Honduras una tarde,
                agosto 5,
(y ya no pasará un 5 de agosto sin que recuerden
aquella marcha hacia Trujillo con la luna menguante).
Salía el alba tras las palmeras
cuando llegaron
      con el grito agudo de los centinelas
al fuerte de murallas manchadas y cañones plateados.
Y tomaron el fuerte.
Las casas eran de piedra, de un piso, y con tejas rojas
sostenidas por cañas sobre grandes vigas,
y muchas iguanas grandes en las tejas.

At last the pure waters,
the clean blue breezes of the early morning
and out of Granada with its red corpses and torches
and groans and death rattles and shouts and explosions
and the smell of the houses, rags, furniture, garbage, bodies burning!
Toward the two brother volcanos
rising out of the waters,
and through the closed-off villages
                    with the dogs barking . . .
And the men went back to the States.

I stayed in the country for a while, living in León.
And Bill Deshon, Shipley, Dixie, Bob Gray, Bill Stoker,
and others came to see me
and they told me about the second expedition
                    and Walker's death.

How on the Mississippi one night he silently weighed anchor:
They landed on the coast of Honduras late in the afternoon,
                    August 5,
(and most likely the 5th of August doesn't go by when they don't think back
on that march to Trujillo with a waning moon).
Dawn was coming up through the palms
when they arrived
        to the sharp cry of the sentries
at the fort with stained ramparts and silvery cannons.
And they took the fort.
The houses were made of stone, with one floor, and red-tiled roofs
held up by cane poles on top of big beams,
and many big iguanas on the roofs.

Allí fue que a Henry,
fumando borracho junto a la pólvora,
le disparó Dolan, entrándole
la bala en la boca,
y Walker corrió a recogerlo,
y Dolan explicando lo que había pasado.
Y Walker se sentó a la cabecera de Henry,
y se hundió el sol y salió la luna
y allí él estaba todavía
y transcurrió toda la noche
y allí él estaba todavía,
humedeciéndole la cara con paños mojados,
y al amanecer salió, y relevó la guardia.
Dolan hablaba de refuerzos
                    pero nunca llegaron.
Y entonces llegó el ultimátum de los ingleses.
Walker entró otra vez y se sentó a la cabecera de Henry.
Henry no podía hablar y tenía una pizarra en que escribía.
Walker cogió la pizarra y escribió unas palabras
y le pasó la pizarra.
Henry se quedó pensando.
Después cogió la pizarra y escribió una palabra.
Walker miró la pizarra.
Se quedó largo tiempo pensando,
                    y salió.
Gusanos le habían comido la mitad de la cara.
En una mesa junto a la cama había una botella que decía
                    "morfina"
y un resto de limonada verde en un vaso.
Y cuando Walker salió, se incorporó,
puso unas cucharadas de la botella en el vaso,
lo revolvío un poco y lo bebió,
se acostó de nuevo,
jaló la rala colcha con cuidado,

It was there that Henry,
drunk, smoking a cigar near the gunpowder,
was shot by Dolan, the bullet hitting him
right in the mouth,
and Walker came quick to gather him up,
as Dolan was explaining how it happened.
And so Walker sat down at Henry's bedside,
and the sun went down, the moon rose
and he was still there
and the whole night went by
and he was still there,
applying wet cloths to Henry's wounded face,
and in the morning he left, and relieved the guards.
Dolan spoke of reinforcements
                    but they never did come.
And then came the ultimatum from the British.
Walker entered once more and sat down at Henry's bedside.
Henry couldn't speak, so he had a slate on which he wrote.
Walker took the slate and wrote a few words
and handed him the slate.
Henry was thinking hard.
Then he took the slate and wrote a single word.
Walker glanced at the slate.
He sat still a long time thinking,
                    then left.
Worms had eaten away half of his face.
On a table beside his bed was a bottle marked
                    "morphine"
and part of a glass of green lemonade.
And when Walker left, he sat up,
put a few spoonfuls from the bottle into the glass,
stirred it up a little and drank it,
lay down again,
pulled the thin blanket carefully over himself,

cruzó las manos sobre el pecho
y se durmió.
                    Y no despertó jamás.
Era medianoche cuando llegó Dolan,
vio a Henry y se acercó,
miró la pizarra, leyó la palabra
y dijo:
                    "eso lo explica."
Después marcharon en fila,
con la colcha y el rifle,
en busca del campamento de Cabañas,
porque había sido la palabra de Henry: "Cabañas."
Pasaron un bosque de naranjos.
Marcharon rápidos y en silencio toda la noche,
sin detenerse a enterrar a los muertos.
Hicieron alto en la tarde a la salida de la luna
y se montó una guardia.
Marcharon más noche.
Hicieron alto a la salida del sol
en una plantación de bananos.
Las balas brotaban de las hojas.
Les disparaban cuando se detenían a beber,
                    tras los bananos.
Walker fue herido levemente en una mejilla
(la primera bala que lo hería en un combate).
Y llegaron por fin al campamento de Cabañas
y vieron los fosos y las municiones pero no a Cabañas.
¡Qué largos calientes días fueron aquellos
en los pantanos pegajosos con los pesados rifles
desde el alba hasta las puestas de sol sangrientas y calientes!
Walker con fiebre más pálido que nunca.

Y perdieron la cuenta de los días.
Hasta que un día vieron venir a los ingleses por el río.
El Gen. Walker fue el último en subir a bordo.
                    —¡Todos los que están vivos, señor!

folded his hands on his chest
and went to sleep.
                    And he never woke up.
It was midnight when Dolan came in.
He glanced at Henry and went over,
looked at the slate, read the word,
and said:
                  "that explains it."
Then they marched out in ranks,
each with a blanket and rifle,
in search of Cabañas' camp,
because that had been Henry's word: "Cabañas."
They went through a grove of orange trees.
They marched swiftly and in silence all night,
without stopping to bury their dead.
They halted in the evening for the moon to rise
and a guard was posted.
They marched more by night.
They halted at sunrise
at a banana plantation.
Bullets were bursting from the leaves.
They fired back at them when they stopped to drink,
                     behind banana trees.
Walker was wounded slightly on one cheek
(the first bullet to wound him in a battle).
And they finally reached Cabañas' camp
and found the rifle pits but no Cabañas.
What long, hot days those were
in sticky swamps with heavy rifles
from dawn until the blood-red sundowns hot as hell!
Walker with fever, paler than ever.

And they lost all track of the days.
Until one day they saw the British coming up the river.
General Walker was the last to climb aboard.
        —All that are alive, sir!

Cuando despertaron era de día, anclados en Trujillo,
y arriba el fuerte negro parecía una mueca.
Y pusieron a los heridos bajo toldos de lona.

A Walker lo estaban juzgando en el fuerte.
Lo vieron pasar después rodeado de guardias,
pálido como siempre,
y podían ver la cicatriz, más pálida, en su mejilla.
Llevaba un crucifijo en la mano.

Cuando hicieron alto
el oficial que comandaba la guardia
leyó un papel en español,
                seguramente las órdenes.
Y entonces Walker, con la voz calma y serena,
sin temblor,
habló en español.
Y los filibusteros no oyeron lo que decía.
Podían ver desde donde estaban
una fosa cavada en la arena,
y a Walker junto a la fosa, que seguía hablando
                calmo y sereno.
Y el hombre dijo:
                "El Presidente
el Presidente de Nicaragua, es nicaragüense..."
Hubo un toque de tambor
y una descarga.
Todas las balas hicieron blanco.
De noventa y uno solo doce volvieron.
Y allí quedó sin coronas ni epitafio junto al mar
William Walker de Tennessee.

It was daylight when they woke up, at anchor at Trujillo,
and it looked like a grimace hung above the black fort.
And they put the wounded under sailcloth awnings.

In the fort they were court-martialing Walker.
They saw him pass by the next morning surrounded by guards,
his face pale as always,
and they could see the scar, paler, on his cheek.
He carried a crucifix in his hand.

When they halted
the officer commanding the guard
read a paper in Spanish,
              surely his orders.
And then Walker, in a calm and dignified voice,
without trembling,
spoke in Spanish.
And the filibusters didn't hear what he said.
They could see from where they stood
a newly made grave in the sand,
and Walker, who kept speaking, calm and dignified,
              beside the grave.
And the man said:
              "The President
the President of Nicaragua, is a Nicaraguan..."
There was a drum roll
and gunfire.
All the bullets hit the mark.
Out of ninety-one men only twelve made it back.
And there, by the sea, with no wreaths or epitaph remained
William Walker of Tennessee.

Los filibusteros

Hubo rufianes, ladrones, jugadores, pistoleros.
También hubo honrados y caballeros y valientes.
Reclutados por la necesidad y las ilusiones:
Uno estaba una mañana sin empleo en un muelle,
y llegaba un agente de Walker con un pasaje gratis
a Nicaragua.
           —Hacia donde no había pasaje de vuelta.
O vinieron por 160 acres de tierra de Centro América
(para venderla) y 25 dólares al mes,
y pelearon por nada al mes, y seis pies cuadrados de tierra.
O venían en busca de gloria: un nombre
que quedara escrito en las páginas de la Historia.
Y sus nombres quedaron olvidados,
en cuarteles con las tablas arrancadas para los ataúdes
y el sargento borracho, chanchos, excremento;
o en aquellos hospitales de mangos, cocos y almendras
donde deliraban delante de los congos y las urracas
con los escalofríos del viento del Lago.
Y fueron más afortunados los que murieron en batallas
o en emboscadas de noche en caminos extraños como un sueño,
o por accidentes o muerte violenta.
Y siempre venía cargada de más filibusteros
y más filibusteros,
para San Juan del Sur
           y para San Juan del Norte,
"La Compañía del Tránsito"
           como una barca de Caronte.
Vanderbilt y Morgan sabían adónde veníamos
           (casi todos murieron)
y les robaban en Nicaragua el dinero a los muertos.

The Filibusters

There were scoundrels, thieves, gamblers, gunslingers.
There were also honest men and gentlemen and brave men.
Fellows enlisting out of necessity and illusions:
Some fellow out of work one morning would be on a pier,
and an agent of Walker would come up with a free passage
to Nicaragua.
                    —Toward where there was no passage back.
Or they came for 160 acres of land in Central America
(to sell it) and 25 bucks a month,
and they fought for nothing a month, and six square feet of earth.
Or they'd come in search of glory: a name
forever written down in the pages of History.
And their names were forgotten,
in barracks with boards taken out to make their coffins
and the drunken sergeant, pigs, crap;
or in those hospitals consisting of mango, coconut and almond groves
where they suffered from delirium with howler monkeys and magpies all around
getting chills from the wind off the Lake.
And the luckiest ones were those who died in battles
or in ambushes at night along strange roads like a dream,
or by accidents or sudden death.
And always loaded with more filibusters
and more filibusters,
bound for San Juan del Sur
                          and for San Juan del Norte,
the "Transit Company" would come
                    like Charon's boat.
Vanderbilt and Morgan knew where we were going
                                (almost all died)
and down in Nicaragua they stole money from the dead.

Joaquín Artola

Yo ya trabajé una vez en esta hacienda, patrón,
cuando la guerra—dice el campisto—.
Yo era muchacho, y me acuerdo que una mañana
todavía bien temprano y con el llano todo nublado
salí a recoger la yeguada para tusarla,
y ya venía con las yeguas cuando oigo unos tiros
y las yeguas que oyen los tiros y se asustan
y yo las chuceo para que no se me vuelvan
y las bestias se me corren y yo voy detrás dellas,
y eran los yankis, que cuando oyeron la yeguada
huyeron por el llano creyendo que eran refuerzos
y yo a caballo detrás de las yeguas y los yankis
y los voy chuzando a los yankis y gritando:
¡Ansina que aquí soy yo, Joaquín Artola!
Y detrás de mí los otros los van macheteando
o lazándolos con soga y guindándolos de los palos
y un Andrés Castro mató a uno con una piedra.
Los demás se corrieron por el llano de Ostocal.
Hoy vuelvo aquí, ya viejo, a pedir trabajo, patrón,
pero no es la primera vez que yo estoy en "San Jacinto."

Joaquín Artola

I spent time working on this ranch once before, boss,
during the war, the peasant says.
I was a boy, and I remember how one morning
pretty early yet and with the plain all cloudy
I went out to fetch the mares to shear them,
and soon I was coming in with them when I hear some shots
and hearing the shots the mares get frightened
and I prod them to keep them from turning around on me
and the beasts get away from me and I go chasing after them,
and there were the Yankees, who when they heard the drove of horses
fled across the plain thinking they were reinforcements
and I'm riding behind the horses and the Yankees
and goading the Yankees and shouting:
So here I am, Joaquín Artola!
And behind me the others are wounding them with machetes
or roping them with lassos and using sticks to club them
and a fellow named Andrés Castro killed one with a rock.
The rest ran off across the Ostocal Plain.
Today I'm back here, an old man now, to ask for work, boss,
but this is not the first time that I am at "San Jacinto."

(*Note:* The Battle of San Jacinto was the turning point in the Filibuster War of 1855–57. The
defenders at San Jacinto dealt Walker his first defeat in battle, and are revered today as national
heroes in Nicaragua.)

José Dolores Estrada

(A todos los exiliados nicaragüenses)

Peleó contra el gobierno español en las calles de Xalteva
en la fracasada rebelión de Abril de 1812.
Pero no fue suya la gloria. El era un muchacho entonces,
y los cabecillas fueron otros.
Después derrotó a los yankis en la hacienda San Jacinto.
El era el general entonces. Pero no fue sólo suya la gloria.
Los soldados y los campistos también pelearon.
Ya viejo, en el exilio, por oponerse a la reelección
del Presidente (su amigo íntimo)
escribe a sus amigos desde Costa Rica:

"Yo estoy aquí haciendo un limpiecito
para ver si puedo sembrar unas matas de tabaco."

Y esa fue su gloria mayor:
porque fue su batalla más dura, y en la que él peleó solo,
sin general, ni soldados, ni trompetas, ni victoria.

José Dolores Estrada

(To all the exiled Nicaraguans)

He fought against the Spanish governor in the streets of Xalteva
in the unsuccessful rebellion of April 1812.
But the glory wasn't his. He was a boy then,
and other rebels were the leaders.
He later defeated the Yankees at the San Jacinto ranch.
He was general then. But the glory wasn't just his.
Soldiers and peasants fought too.
Now an old man, in exile, for opposing the re-election
of the President (his close friend)
he writes to his friends from Costa Rica:

"I am clearing a little patch here
to see if I can grow some tobacco plants."

And that was his great glory:
because it was his hardest battle, and the one in which he fought alone,
with no general, or soldiers, or trumpets, or victory.

Greytown

¡Greytown! ¡Greytown!
Americanos, alemanes, irlandeses,
franceses, mulatos, chinos, españoles,
venían, se encontraban aquí, y partían.
What's the news from New York? New Orleans? Havanah?
Pagaban guayabas con marcos; una botella de ron
con dólares, francos, libras esterlinas.
                        Any new annexation?
Y quebrando el reflejo del follaje
               se alejaba el "Daniel Webster". . .

Edwards E. Brand, de Kentucky, fue el último norteamericano
que se quedó en Greytown, esperando el Canal.
Esperó el Canal toda su vida. Y vivió un siglo:
Vestido siempre con saco, chaleco, corbata y sombrero de pita.
En los últimos años los vecinos le daban de comer,
ya no tenía zapatos y andaba descalzo,
pero siempre con saco, chaleco, corbata y sombrero de pita.

¡Greytown! ¡Greytown! Ciudad Gris.
Ahora sólo hay arena gris y mar gris bajo el cielo gris.
Cascos de buques viejos en la costa seca.
Chozas de paja seca bajo los cocos secos.
Sol sobre salinas secas. Sal de color de ceniza.
Salinas planas. Playa plana. Y mar plano.
Todo tan húmedo. Todo tan estéril. Todo tan verde.
Una draga sarrosa junto al mar.
Una fragata entre el zacate
             (con el cordaje de lianas).
En la Plaza King George pacen las vacas.
Un siglo de desolación ha pasado como un lento ciclón.
De noche el mar sucio ladra como un perro

Greytown

Greytown! Greytown!
Americans, Germans, Irishmen,
Frenchmen, mulattoes, Chinamen, Spaniards,
they'd all come, meet each other here, and leave.
What's the news from New York? New Orleans? Havana?
They paid for guavas with marks; a bottle of rum
with dollars, francs, pounds.
                    Any new annexation?
And breaking up the reflection of leaves
            the "Daniel Webster" would pull away...

Edwards E. Brand, from Kentucky, was the last North American
who stayed in Greytown, waiting for the Canal.
He waited for the Canal his whole life. And he lived a century:
Always dressed in a coat, vest, necktie and straw hat.
In his last years his neighbors used to feed him,
he no longer had shoes and went around barefoot,
but always in a coat, vest, necktie and straw hat.

Greytown! Greytown!
Now there's only grey sand and a grey sea under grey skies.
Hulls of old ships on the dry seashore.
Huts made of dried cane under dry coconut palms.
Sun on dry salt marshes. Salt the color of ash.
Flat salt marshes. Flat beach. And a flat sea.
All so humid. All so barren. All so green.
A rusty dredge beside the sea.
A frigate lying in the grass
                    (with rigging of vines).
In King George Square cows graze.
A century of desolation has passed like a slow cyclone.
At night the foul sea bays like a dog

hurgando huesos, palos secos, latas y botellas.
El viento del mar avienta la arena caliente
contra las tucas secas, los semi-enterrados
rieles corroídos, los viejos vagones vacíos,
la vieja Aduana de zinc sarrosa y vacía.
¡Y pareciera de pronto que un gran barco con sus mástiles
se viniera abriendo paso en la selva!
En la Calle Green aúlla un mono bajo la luna.
En la playa brillan grandes cerros de botellas . . .

stirring up bones, withered sticks, cans and bottles.
The wind from the sea throws hot sand
against the dry logs, the corroded
half-buried train tracks, the empty old cars,
the empty and rust-caked old Custom House.
And suddenly it would seem that a great ship with its masts
was cutting right through the jungle!
On Green Street a monkey howls under the moon.
On the beach big heaps of bottles gleam...

Squier en Nicaragua

Verdes tardes de la selva; tardes
tristes. Río verde
entre zacatales verdes;
pantanos verdes.
Tardes olorosas a lodo, a hojas mojadas, a
helechos húmedos y a hongos.
El verde perezoso cubierto de moho
poco a poco trepando de rama en
rama, con los ojos cerrados como
dormido pero comiendo
una hoja, alargando un garfio primero
y después el otro,
sin importarle las hormigas que le pican,
volteando lentamente el bobo rostro
redondo, primero a un lado
y luego al otro,
enrollando por fin la cola en una rama
y colgándose pesado como
una bola de plomo;
el salto del sábalo en el río;
el griterío de los monos comiendo
malcriadamente, a toda prisa,
arrojándose las cáscaras de anona unos a otros
y peleándose, charlando, arremedándose
y riéndose entre los árboles;
monas chillonas cargando a tuto monitos
pelones y trompudos;
la guatuza bigotuda y elástica
que se estira y encoge
mirando a todos lados con su ojo redondo
mientras come temblando;

Squier in Nicaragua

Green afternoons in the jungle; sad
afternoons. A green river
going through green pastures;
green marshes.
Afternoons that smell of mud, rain-soaked leaves, of
wet ferns and mushrooms.
The green, moss-covered sloth
little by little climbing from branch to
branch, with its eyes closed as if
asleep but eating
a leaf, stretching out one front claw
followed by the other,
not bothered at all by the ants biting it,
slowly turning its round funny-looking
face, first to one side
and then the other,
finally wrapping its tail around a branch
and hanging down heavily like
a ball of lead;
the shad leaping in the river;
the din of monkeys eating
ill-manneredly, quick as they can,
throwing soursop peels at each other
and fighting, chattering, mimicking one another
and laughing in the trees;
screeching female monkeys carrying pickaback
bald babies with lips flared;
the elastic long-whiskered agouti
that stretches and shrinks up
looking all around with its round eye
while it eats, trembling;

espinosas iguanas
como dragones de jade
corriendo sobre el agua
(¡flechas de jade!);
el negro con su camisa rayada, remando
en su canoa de ceiba.

Una muchacha meciéndose en una hamaca,
con su largo pelo negro, y una pierna desnuda
colgando de la hamaca,
nos saluda:
        "Adios, California!"

El río negro, como tinta, al anochecer.
Una flor de un hedor putrefacto
                como un cadáver;
y una flor horrible, peluda.
              Orquídeas
guindadas sobre el agua podrida.
Silbidos tristes de la selva,
y quejidos.
        Quejidos.
Hojas tristes que caen dando vueltas.
Y chillidos...
        ¡Un grito entre las guanábanas!
El hacha cortando un tronco
        y el eco del hacha.
¡El mismo chillido!
Ruido sordo de manadas de cerdos salvajes.
¡Carcajadas!
        El canto de un tucán.

spiny iguanas
like jade dragons
shooting over the water
(jade arrows!):
the black man with his striped shirt, paddling
in his ceiba canoe.

A girl swinging to and fro in a hammock,
with long black hair, and a bare leg
hanging out of the hammock,
greets us:
                    "Adios, California!"

The black river, like ink, at dusk.
Some flower with a sickening stench
                              like a corpse;
and a horrible flower, all hairy.
                         Orchids
hanging over stagnant water.
Sad whistles in the jungle,
and moans.
              Moans.
Sad leaves that fall spinning around.
And screeches...
                    A cry among the *guanabanas*!
An ax chopping a log
                    and the echo of the ax.
The same screeching!
Packs of wild pigs grunting.
Outbursts of laughter!
                    The song of a toucan.

Chischiles de culebras cascabeles.
Gritos de congos.
                    Chachalacas.
El canto melancólico de la gongolona
                    entre los coquitales,
y el de la paloma poponé,
                    poponé, poné, poné.
Oropéndolas sonoras
columpiándose en sus nidos colgados de las palmeras,
y el canto del pájaro-león entre los coyoles
y el del pájaro de-la-luna-y-el-sol
y el pájaro clarinero, el pájaro
relojero que da la hora
y el pocoyo que canta de noche (o caballero)
                    Cabayero mi dinero   Cabayero mi dinero
parejas de lapas que pasan gritando,
y el güis, chichitote y dichoso-fui
                    dichoso-fuiiiiiiií
que cantan en los chagüites sombríos.
Plateados pantanos rielando,
y las ranas cantando
                    rrrrrrrrrrrrr
¡Y un pájaro que toda la noche repite a gritos su nombre!

El sol poniéndose detrás del Orosí: el Orosí
rosa, el cielo carmesí, y fuego el Archipiélago
de Las Solentinames, flotando en agua de oro,
y rosa el lago después, y después ópalo, y verdes
las palmeras de las islas contra el cielo,
y el cielo gris después, y el agua gris;
y en el cielo de la tarde brilla una estrella triste.
Los remeros cantan:
                    Ave María Purísima. . .
y después un silencio;

Rattling of rattlesnakes.
Cries of howler monkeys.
                              Chachalacas.
The melancholy song of the *gongolona*
                              among coquito palms,
and the song of the dove "go-go-lay,
                              go-go-lay, go-lay, go-lay."
Songful golden orioles
swaying in their nests suspended from palm trees,
and the song of the lion bird in the cohune palms
and the song of the moon-and-sun bird
and the bugler bird, the clock
bird singing out the hour
and the potoo that sings at night (oh poor me)
                              "Poor-me-one"   "Poor-me-one"
pairs of macaws that pass by squawking,
and the *güis, chichitote* and "feeling-joy"
                              "feeling-joyyyyyyyy"
which they sing in among the gloomy bogs.
Silvery marshes all aglow,
and the frogs singing
                              rrrrrrrrrrrrr
And a bird that all night long keeps calling its name!

The sun setting behind Orosí: Orosí
rose-colored, the sky crimson, and the fiery Archipelago
of the Solentinames, floating in liquid gold,
and the lake then rose-colored, and then opal, and the green
palm trees on the islands against the sky,
and the sky then gray, and the water gray;
and a sad star shines in the evening sky.
The oarsmen sing:
                              Ave María purísima . . .
and then a silence;

                              sólo
las olas del lago en la noche tranquila.
                    La luna sobre el lago
y las siluetas de las palmeras negras bajo la luna.

Sólo el golpe del agua contra el bongo.

La isla de Ometepe: el agua verde bajo la isla.
En el agua una lancha inclinada con las velas recogidas.
En la isla, ropa de todos colores tendida en la playa.
Una carreta con sus bueyes bebiendo agua.
Un muchacho desnudo bañando un caballo.
Y los indios acarreando leña, pequeñitos.
Detrás los ranchos grises.
Cocos de color de oro.
Y arriba el volcán verde
echando una bocanada de humo indolentemente
                              en el viento azul.

El lago azul.
La garza blanca.
                    Y una vela blanca lejana.

Isletas verdes, con rocas negras y con
icacos, platanales, palmeras y papayas,
y ranchos de paja entre los platanales.
                              Donde
las campánulas amarillas de las "gloria-de-Nicaragua"
colgadas de los árboles
y resbalando por las rocas
                    se columpiaban sobre el agua.

                    just
the waves of the lake in the peaceful night.
                    The moon above the lake
and the silhouette of dark palms in the moonlight.

Just the water beating against our bungo.

The island of Ometepe: the water green below the island.
In the water a launch leaning with its sails rolled up.
On the island, clothes of every color spread out on the beach.
A cart with its oxen drinking water.
A naked boy bathing his horse.
And Indians (quite short) carrying firewood.
Behind gray huts.
Gold-colored coconuts.
And up above the green volcano
blowing out a lazy puff of smoke
                              into the blue air.

The blue lake.
The white heron.
                    And a white sail in the distance.

Green islets, with black rocks and
icacos, plantain groves, palms and papayas,
and cane huts among the plantain groves.
                              Where
the yellow bellflowers of the "gloria de Nicaragua"
hanging from trees
and trailing over rocks
                    would sway above the water.

Y en el espejo del agua
invertidas las isletas verdes
con las rocas negras y los icacos
platanales, palmeras y papayas.
Un bote negro atado a la orilla del agua;
en el agua una mujer con los pechos desnudos
y una falda de púrpura,
lavando ropa en una roca blanca,
con el agua hasta las rodillas;
y el largo pelo lacio le caía suelto hasta el agua;
y la falda de púrpura,
los pechos desnudos,
el pelo negro,
el bote negro,
           reflejados en el agua.
Y lejos
la silueta de un bote con dos personas
           doblando una isla.

La primera noche en Granada: Granada
en estado de sitio; y cada 2 minutos
durante toda la noche, gritaban *¡Alerta!*
(Y yo soñé esa noche con tormentas en el lago.
Las iguanas caminando sobre el Río Frío
y los marineros cantaban La Salve
y Bernabé Somoza asaltaba Granada...)
Sobre los tejados de Granada
aquel verdor deslumbrante:
           —como un fuego que fuese verde.
Y los primeros faroles
        pálidos, en el crepúsculo.
Una polka en un piano lejano.

And in that mirror of water
upside down, the green islets
with their black rocks and their icacos
plantain groves, palms and papayas.
A black boat lashed to the shore;
in the water a woman with bare breasts
and a purple skirt,
washing clothes on a white rock,
and water up to her knees;
and her long straight hair was falling freely to the water;
and her purple skirt,
bare breasts,
black hair,
black boat,
                    reflected in the water.
And far off
the silhouette of a boat with two people
                            rounding an island.

The first night in Granada: Granada
under siege; and throughout the night
every 2 minutes they shouted *Alerta!*
(And that night I dreamt of storms on the lake.
Iguanas walking over Rio Frio
and the sailors were singing the Salve
and Bernabe Somoza was attacking Granada...)
On the tiled roofs of Granada
that dazzling verdure:
                    —like a fire burning green.
And the first street lamps
            pale, in the twilight.
A polka on a distant piano.

Y entre el olor de narcisos
sube una canción desde un patio:
                            Delgadina, levantáte
                            ponéte el vestido blanco.
Y un repique de campanas
                claras y roncas
                y claras y claras
                        (clin-clan, clin-clan)
hierro ronco alternando con hierros claros:
                        —¡es el toque del Angelus!

Nindirí:
¡Cómo describirte a ti,
Nindirí,
¡linda Nindirí!
Bajo bóvedas verdes:
avenidas; las avenidas
bien barridas de Nindirí.
Chozas sencillas, de paja,
bajo el ramaje verde,
como nidos.
Nindirí:
el nombre musical que te dieron a ti
cuando Roma era joven todavía
(*Ninda,* agua; y *Diria,* tierra)
nos habla en una lengua antigua y olvidada
de la laguna y el volcán.
Nindirí, linda Nindirí:
naranjas, bananos de oro, icacos,
oro entre las hojas.
Muchachas de color de chocolate
con los pechos desnudos
hilando algodón blanco entre los árboles.
Tranquila y primitiva Nindirí,

And amid the smell of narcissus
a song rises from a courtyard:

> *Delgadina, get up and*
> *put on your white dress.*

And a peal of bells
      clear and harsh
      and clear and clear
           (cling-clang, cling-clang)
a harsh iron sound alternating with clear iron sounds:
           —it's the tolling of the Angelus!

Nindirí!
How shall I describe you,
Nindirí
beautiful Nindirí!
Beneath green vaults:
avenues; the smooth
avenues of Nindirí.
Simple huts, made out of cane,
under the green branches,
like nests.
Nindirí:
the musical name which they gave you
when Rome was still young
(*Neenda*, water; and *Diria*, mountain)
tells us in an ancient, forgotten tongue
of the lake and the volcano.
Nindirí, beautiful Nindirí:
oranges, golden bananas, icaco plums,
gold among the leaves.
Girls the color of chocolate,
their breasts bare,
spinning white cotton among the trees.
Quiet primitive Nindirí,

sede de los antiguos caciques y sus cortes,
¡visión de la noche, Arcadia de ensueño,
irreal!
¡Cómo olvidarme de ti!
La laguna en el cráter, como en una copa,
y lavanderas lavando en la laguna.
La lava: como un mar de hierro derretido,
un mar de roca roja, sin un árbol,
tormenta petrificada, remolinos, olas
sobre olas, filosas como cuchillos.

Jacintos lilas y blancos de las fincas;
y la flor del malinche, la flor
sacuanjoche,
en los colochos y trenzas de color azabache.
Sonrisas de las bocas pintadas de achiote.
Y las muchachas de Masaya,
con sus rojas tinajas y porongas
                        y sus güipiles blancos.

—Rectas como granaderos
                bajo los cántaros de agua...

                Y sin más velo
que la espuma y el agua rosa,
enchándose el agua con guacales,
y el pelo flotando en el agua...

Mandolinas y luna en los balcones.
Marimbas. Marimbas de Monimbó.
¡Laguna plateada bajo la luna!

seat of the ancient caciques and their courts,
—vision of the night, some dreamy Arcadia,
unreal!
How shall I forget you!
That small lake in the crater, as if in a goblet,
and the women washing clothes in the lake.
The lava: like a sea of molten iron,
a sea of red rock, treeless,
a storm turned to stone, swirls, waves
upon waves, knife-sharp.

White and light purple hyacinths on the farms:
the flower of the *malinche,* the *sacuanjoche*
flower,
in their curls and braids black as jet.
Smiles on lips rouged with annatto.
And the girls of Masaya,
with their large red earthen jars and pots
                    and their white sleeveless blouses.

—Straight as grenadiers
            under the water jars...

                And with no more covering
than the foam and rose-colored water,
splashing water on themselves with gourds,
and their hair floating in the water...

Mandolins and moonlight on balconies.
Marimbas. Marimbas of Monimbó.
A lagoon silver-looking in the moonlight!

Y mujeres morenas de Nindirí
saludaban sonrientes en las puertas de sus ranchos
al viajero que pasaba:
                "*Adiós, americano!*"

Amaneceres borrosos y grises
olorosos a leche y a estiércol verde y a zacate seco
con mugidos de vacas y de terneros tiernos,
y el zanate cantando sobre la vaca.
Ranchos secos, humeantes, en el campo seco.
O ranchos húmedos, hierba verde llovida,
y casas blancas con tejados rojos mojados
bajo el cielo celeste.
Las luciérnagas pálidas de la tarde
y la cigarra triste,
las cigarras,
y la carreta
y el canto del carretero.
Y el zanate cantando sobre la cerca.

"Adiós, Señores"
                "Buen viaje, Caballero"

Había siempre en los caminos una cruz
con flores secas...

Y la lucecita en el monte, y el ladrido lejano.
Y las quemas lejanas de los cerros.

Una campana oída tras de las ceibas
con un sonido ensarrado:
        Es la hora de la Oración
                y estamos junto a Managua.

And those dark-skinned women of Nindirí
smiling in the doorways of their huts would greet
the passing traveler:
> *"Adios, americano!"*

Cloudy gray dawns
smelling of milk and fresh manure and dried hay
with the lowing of cows and young calves,
and the *zanate* (a native bird) singing on a cow.
Dry huts, smoking, in the dry countryside.
Or wet huts, green rain-soaked grass,
and white houses with red-tiled roofs drenched
under the light blue sky.
Pale fireflies around evening time
and the sad cicada,
cicadas,
and the cart
and the song of the cart driver.
And the *zanate* singing on a fence.

"Good-bye, Gentlemen"
> *"Have a good trip, Sir"*

On the roads there was always a cross
with dried flowers . . .

And the tiny light in the brush, and the barking far off.
And fires far off in the hills.

A bell heard from behind the ceiba trees
with a piercing sound:
> It's the hour for Vespers
>> and we are near Managua.

Las muchachas de Managua
bajaban todas las tardes cantando a la costa del Lago
a llenar sus cántaros de agua.
                Sardinas de plata saltaban en el agua.

Mediodía junto al lago de Managua:
Inmóvil en el cielo el humo del Momotombo.
Un zopilote parado en mitad de su vuelo.
Y el sol alumbra sin proyectar sombra.

Las dos muchachas de Buena Vista:
        "La blanquita" y "la negrita."
                "Buena Vista," Caballeros!
Este hato se llama "Santa María de Buena Vista"!
Éstos son mis niños pequeños
y aquéllas mis hijas grandes!
Una era blanca con el pelo rubio y los ojos azules
        y la otra morena.
                La negrita es hija de mi marido
                y la otra de un francés!
Y loras verdes entre los árboles.
Una casita de paja
rodeada de palmeras y de plátanos.
                Caballeros, yo fui joven una vez . . .
Y las dos cabecitas juntas asomadas en la puerta
y los chiquillos desnudos, asustados.
Adiós, amigas!
                Dios guarde a Ustedes, caballeros!
"Califooooooornia?"

The girls of Managua
toward evening would go singing down to the lake shore
to fill their water jars.
        Silvery sardines were leaping up in the water.

Noon by Lake Managua:
The smoke from Momotombo just hanging in the sky.
A buzzard stopped in the middle of its flight.
And the sun shining down without throwing a shadow.

The two girls of Buena Vista:
      "The white one" and "the black one."
            "Buena Vees-ta," Gentlemen!
This here farm is called "Santa Maria de Buena Vista"!
These are my little boys
and those my big girls!
One was white with light hair and blue eyes
      and the other dark-skinned.
          The black one is my husband's daughter
          and the other one a Frenchman's!
And green parrots in the trees.
A cane hut
surrounded by palm and plantain trees.
          Gentlemen, I was young once...
And two little heads together sticking out of the doorway
and the kids naked, frightened.
Good-bye, sweethearts!
          God preserve you, Gentlemen!
"Califoooooornia?"

Hileras uniformes de palmeras
y al final de las plantaciones de caña
un techo rojo.
El humo azul del ingenio,
el olor a guarapo,
              y una hamaca meciéndose.
Un molino monótono
              a punto de pararse en cada vuelta.
En el sol, una carreta cargada de leña,
arrastrada por dos bueyes dormidos.
                    Arre, arre jodido.
En la pared, un rifle,
un retrato de Lola Montes
y un cuero de tigre.
Y en el aire, el vuelo de una mosca como un hilo.
Los zopilotes dando vueltas en el cielo.
Y la hamaca meciéndose.
              Y la soñolienta molienda de caña.
Arre Canelo.

Una cruz verde junto a una fuente,
adornada con guirnaldas secas,
y un niño sentado al pie de la cruz.
Y le pregunté por qué estaba allí aquella cruz:
Recordaba un crimen horrible, me dijo.
Y no supe otra cosa de esa cruz,
sino que la víctima era una mujer.

Even rows of palm trees
and at the end of the cane fields
a red roof.
The blue steam from the mill,
the smell of sugar-cane juice,
    and a hammock swinging to and fro.
A monotonous mill
    just about to stop at each turn.
In the sun, a cart loaded up with firewood,
pulled by two sleepy oxen.
    Giddyap, giddyap you bastard.
On the wall, a rifle,
a portrait of Lola Montez
and a tiger skin.
And in the air, the flight of a fly like a thread.
Buzzards circling in the sky.
And the hammock swinging to and fro.
    And that drowsy milling of sugar cane.
Giddyap Canelo.

A green cross next to a spring,
decorated with dried wreaths,
and a little boy sitting at the foot of the cross.
And so I asked him why that cross was there:
It commemorated a horrible crime, he said.
And I learned nothing else about the cross,
except that the victim was a woman.

Viajero del Siglo XIX en el Río San Juan

El bongo mudo bogaba por el río
bordeando de nenúfares y juncos
                    (del ancho del Sena frente al Louvre).
Los pájaros ya no cantaban
y todo era silencio y verdura sin fin y soledades sin eco.
A las 6 vino la noche sin crepúsculo.
Sólo se oía el rumor de los remos en el río...
Y mis ideas se fueron llenando de sombras,
                                y me dormí.

Cuando desperté el bongo estaba inmóvil en la oscuridad.
Estábamos atados al tronco de un árbol.
Miles de luciérnagas en el follaje negro
y al fondo del cielo negro
                    la Cruz del Sur...
Y hubo un ruido en el aire:
el grito tal vez de un pájaro desconocido,
respondido por otro grito semejante más lejos.
¡Sarapiquí!:
El agua tan clara
que no se veía.
Dos riberas verdes
                y las riberas al revés.
Cielo azul arriba
                y cielo abajo.
        Y el agua en medio, no se veía.

19th-Century Traveler on the Río San Juan

The silent bungo was oared up the river
bordered by water lilies and rushes
         (as wide as the Seine in front of the Louvre).
The birds quit singing,
and all was quietness and endless verdure and echoless retreats.
At 6 o'clock night came without twilight.
Only the plash of oars in the river was heard...
And my thoughts filled with shadows,
                and I fell asleep.

When I awoke the bungo was motionless in the dark.
We were tied up to the trunk of a tree.
Thousands of fireflies in the black foliage
and the Southern Cross
             deep in the black sky...
And there was a clamor in the air:
the cry perhaps of a strange bird,
answering another cry like it farther off.
Sarapiquí!:
The water so clear
it was invisible.
Two green riverbanks
         and the riverbanks upside down.
Blue sky above
        and sky below.
     And the water in between, invisible.

Había una casa blanca con barandas verdes
que resaltaba entre el verde-tierno de los bananales
y una vela triangular, sucia y zurcida,
temblaba en espera, inflada ya por la brisa,
junto a las gradas que bajaban hasta el agua.
Una mujer vestida de blanco
cruzó tras la baranda, nos miró un instante
                        y desapareció entre los bananales.

There was a white house with green railings
which stood out amid the fresh greenness of the banana groves
and a triangular sail, soiled and patched,
shook in anticipation, blown out by the breeze,
next to the harrows which were set down by the water.
A woman dressed in white
crossed behind the railing, looked at us for a moment
and vanished into the banana groves.

Acuarela

Los ranchos dorados cercados de cardos;
chanchos en las calles;
                    una rueda de carreta
junto a un rancho, un excusado en el patio,
una muchacha llenando su tinaja,
                    y el Momotombo
azul, detrás de los alegres calzones colgados
        amarillos, blancos, rosados.

Watercolor

Golden huts fenced with thistles;
pigs in the streets;
                        a cartwheel
beside a hut, an outhouse in the yard,
a girl filling her water jar,
                        and Momotombo
blue, behind the bright pants hanging out
            yellow, white, pink.

(*Note:* Momotombo, the most famous of Nicaragua's volcanoes, is a
4,199–foot perfect cinder cone on a peninsula thrust into Lake Managua.)

León

Yo vivía en una casa grande junto a la iglesia de San Francisco
que tenía una leyenda en el zaguán que decía
                    AVE MARIA
y rojos corredores de ladrillos de barro,
viejas tejas rojas,
                        y ventanas de rejas ensarradas,
y un gran patio angustioso en las tardes sin aire
con un alcaraván triste que cantaba las horas,
y una tía blanca en el patio rezando el rosario.
En las tardes se oía aquel toque del Angelus
            (*"El Angel del Señor anunció a María..."*)
la mano de una niña lejana tocando una nota de piano,
            y el clarín de un cuartel.
De noche una enorme luna roja subía del Calvario.
Me contaban cuentos de ánimas en pena y aparecidos.
            A media noche
la sombra del general Arechabala cabalgaba por las calles.
Y el ruido de una puerta que se cierra... Un coche negro...
Una carreta vacía corriendo, traqueteando, por la Calle Real.
Y después todos los gallos del vecindario cantando,
y el canto del alcaraván,
y mi tía que salía cada día a su misa de 4
con las campanas repicando en San Francisco,
            repicando
en el Calvario
                    y en el Hospicio de San Juan
y las pichingas de los lecheros chocando en el empedrado
y un panadero golpeando en un zaguán
y gritando
            EL PAN
                    EL PAN

León

I used to live in a big house by the Church of St. Francis
which had an inscription in the entrance hall saying
                    AVE MARIA
and red corridors of brick,
an old red-tiled roof,
                            and windows with rusty iron grilles,
and a large courtyard just unbearable on stuffy afternoons
with a sad clock bird singing out the hours,
and someone's pale aunt in the courtyard reciting the rosary.
In the evenings I'd hear that angelus bell
            (*"The Angel of the Lord declared unto Mary . . ."*)
the hand of a distant little girl playing a note on the piano,
                and the bugle from some barracks.
At night a huge red moon rose above Calvary
They told me stories of souls in purgatory and ghosts.
                    At midnight
the shade of General Arechabala rode a horse through the streets.
And the noise of a door closing . . . A black coach . . .
An empty cart rattling as it rolled through the Calle Real.
And then all the roosters in the neighborhood crowing,
and the song of the clock bird,
and my aunt who'd leave each morning for mass at 4
with the bells ringing in St. Francis,
            ringing
in Calvary
                    and in St. John's Hospital
and the jars of the milkmen clattering on the stone pavement
and a bread vendor knocking on a front door
and crying
            BREAD
                    BREAD

Bibliography: Cardenal in English

Poetry

"Apocalypse" and Other Poems. Translated by Thomas Merton, Robert Pring-Mill, Kenneth Rexroth and Mireya Jaimes-Freyre, and Donald D. Walsh. New York: New Directions, 1977.

Homage to the American Indians. Translated by Monique and Carlos Altschul. Baltimore: Johns Hopkins University Press, 1973.

Marilyn Monroe, and Other Poems. Translated by Robert Pring-Mill. London: Search Press, 1975.

Psalms. Translated by Thomas Blackburn, John Griffiths, John Heath-Stubbs, Sylvester Houédard, Elizabeth Jennings, Peter Levi, and Tony Rudolf. New York: Crossroad, 1981.

The Psalms of Liberation and Struggle. Translated by Amile G. McAnany. New York: Herder & Herder, 1971.

Zero Hour and Other Documentary Poems. Translated by Paul W. Borgeson, Jr., Jonathan Cohen, Robert Pring-Mill, and Donald D. Walsh. New York: New Directions, 1980.

Prose

The Gospel in Solentiname. Translated by Donald D. Walsh. 4 vols. Maryknoll, N.Y.: Orbis Books, 1982.

In Cuba. Translated by Donald D. Walsh. New York: New Directions, 1974.

Love. Translated by Dinah Livingstone. New York: Crossroad, 1981.

To Live Is to Love. Translated by Kurt Reinhardt. New York: Herder & Herder, 1972. Reprint, Garden City, N.Y.: Doubleday, Image Books, 1974.

WESLEYAN POETRY IN TRANSLATION

Elizabeth Bishop, ed. *An Anthology of Twentieth-Century Brazilian Poetry.* Edited, with an introduction, by Elizabeth Bishop and Emanuel Brasil.

Emanuel Brasil and William Jay Smith, eds. *Brazilian Poetry, 1950–1980.*

Gloria Fuertes. *Off the Map: Selected Poems by Gloria Fuertes.* Edited and translated by Philip Levine and Ada Long.

Edmond Jabès. *The Book of Questions.* Translated by Rosmarie Waldrop.

Antonio Machado. *Times Alone: Selected Poems of Antonio Machado.* Translated by Robert Bly.

Norman Shapiro, translator. *Fables from Old French: Aesop's Beasts and Bumpkins.*

About the Author

Ernesto Cardenal is the author of eight books of poetry and several prose works, and since the Sandinist revolution in 1979 he has been Minister of Culture in the Nicaraguan cabinet. From 1947 to 1949 he attended Columbia University, and in 1950 he returned home to write *With Walker in Nicaragua.* In 1952 he received the prize of the Managua Centenary and in 1980 the prestigious Peace Prize of the German Book Trade. His home is in Managua.

About the Translator

Jonathan Cohen has translated and written extensively on Ernesto Cardenal. A graduate of Columbia University (M.F.A., 1976) and the State University of New York at Stony Brook (Ph.D., 1980), he has received grants from the NEA and the NEH, among other awards and fellowships. His translations have appeared in Cardenal's *Zero Hour and Other Documentary Poems* (1980). He is Writer/Editor for the State University of New York at Stony Brook's Department of Surgery and lives in Port Jefferson, N.Y.

About the Book

With Walker in Nicaragua has been composed in Garamond by Marathon Typography Service, Inc., of Durham, North Carolina, and printed on 60 lb. Glatfelter by Braun-Brumfield of Ann Arbor, Michigan. Design by Joyce Kachergis Book Design and Production, Inc., of Bynum, North Carolina. Wesleyan University Press, 1984.